MEN
READ THIS
a spiritual guide for the regular guy

WarriorSage Inc
PO Box 10006
3600 248th Street
Aldergrove, BC V4W 3Z5

ISBN 1-59971-880-4

Dedication

Though my life has been full of 'teachers', I have only recently come to realize the value of the lessons they taught me over the years. These 'teachers' have come in all shapes and sizes. They have brought on all manner of change in me. I have loved them and hated them; I have admired and despised them; I have been happy and angry in their presence; and I have experienced profound bliss and deep rage as a result of them being in my life.

Through the stories in this book I hope to demonstrate how even the darkest crisis in our lives can be used as a brilliant teaching moment. These learning opportunities come our way regularly from birth, even pre-birth and if explored and 'mined' fully can enrich our lives immeasurably. In other words, if we can learn to turn towards the crisis, learn to face it— instead of turning away, we can truly grow and evolve as human beings.

Spiritual Growth for the Regular Guy is a direct result of one such teachable moment in my life; the death of my late sister Johanna Mary Garrett. Her death breathed new life in to my otherwise deadened existence. Her passing, as I turned towards it, inspired me to delve into the Truth of life. And so I did. I have used my personal life experience as a road map for you guys. What I have learned to do has helped me to live an amazing life full of adventure and wonder. What has worked for me can most certainly help you!

I dedicate this book to two remarkable women, my beloved Sonora whose grace and deep love of me inspires me to no end, and to my late sister, Jody, whose love of life and people moves me deeply to this day.

—Stephen

Chapter by Chapter

Encouragement

My intention in writing this book was to help you regular guys understand that personal spiritual growth is available to you. By telling my stories I hope to inspire you to look at your life differently, to look at it from a new perspective—*practical spirituality*.

Most of you tend to turn away from your mistakes, your crises, missing amazing opportunities for your own personal evolution. You tend to blame, point fingers, and generally deflect your upset towards others. You tend to give your personal power away, allowing others to have power over your lives.

This book is a simple example of how to reclaim your personal power—enjoy more passion and fulfillment in your life. I have demonstrated through my stories how you can take responsibility for your life—how you can take the steering wheel of your own car and drive it.

Taking personal responsibility for your life is one of the primary steps in personal spiritual growth in a practical way.

Many men who are truth seekers, often look for ways off the planet, out of their lives and out of their bodies. This book is not that, it is about fully descending into your body, and fully taking the reins of your life NOW. It is about learning to live with passion in an enlightened way. It is about living the life of a Warrior Sage!

If I can do it, so can you!

So just get at it, don't delay! Don't waste any more time waiting for the right moment to start, the right time to change, the right time to grow.

Begin Now.

—Stephen

The Regular Guy's Toolbox for Personal Growth
The Tools and How to Use Them

The Personal Spiritual Growth Wheel

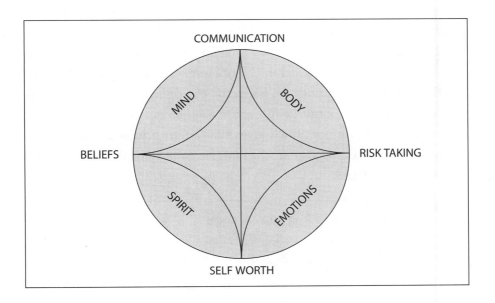

The Personal Spiritual Growth Wheel was inspired by Virginia Satir's work, the Change Wheel, and the Whole Person Circle used in many First Nations healing circles. I have modified them both and combined them in a way that links our inner world, the private self, with the external world of our day to day lives.

The combination of these eight components, four internal and four external, form a dynamic that is interconnected. It is impossible in this model to affect one component without having an affect in the other seven. In a way it is a relief I can work on one section of my life and automatically have a positive affect on my entire life. Unfortunately, it also works in the opposite direction. If I am challenged by some negative events it is just as easy to 'slip' into some old negative reactions and spiral down for some time.

This model will help you understand how these sorts of events, judged by you as positive or negative, can and do affect your entire life. Even though you may put on airs and hold much in, there is still an obvious and immediate effect on those around you and on your whole personhood.

The inner circle, the private self is composed of four linked dynamics. You have likely seen this model in one or more ways. I include in the inner self the following; the mind, the body, the emotions, and the spirit. These four work together to form the full self in each moment. Whether you notice or not these four are always at work. You are always changing from instant to instant as you take in the new, let go of some old and reinforce some that is still there.

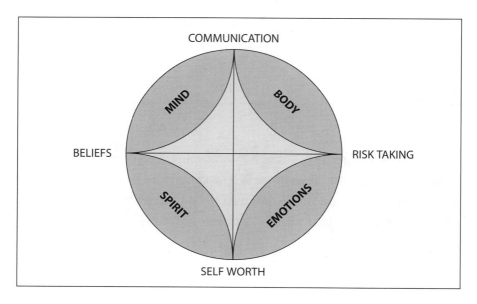

Your mind is a collection of thoughts you have had during your life, including thoughts you have in relation to others. Your mind can be full or empty, relaxed or agitated. Your mind can be the boss, as is generally the case, or your mind can be a tool. The health of your mind is important to the authentic and truthful expression of your life.

An unhealthy mind causes all manner of complications. It can keep you secluded, fear-based, and in a state of withdrawal, over zealous in aggressive expression. A healthy mind is patient, aware and ever present to the events of the moment. Notice the nature of your thoughts. Thoughts can and do turn into reality. What reality are you thinking about?

How healthy is **your body**? Do you eat well? Do you exercise regularly? Do you fuel it with good food and good drink? How does your body reflect your mind? Do you feel at home in your body or would you like to be in someone else's?

It is your body that gets you around in your life. It is the vehicle you drive, the temple you reside in. It is a statement, an expression of how you hold yourself in each moment. Your body is totally linked to your mind, emotions and spirit and can have a huge effect on how you think and behave in the world. Are you well rested? Is your body clean? How does your plumbing work? Any blockages?

By taking the time to notice your body you can learn a lot about yourself, mentally, emotionally and spiritually. Are you steeling yourself against the world and the events life brings you? Check out your forehead, jaw and neck for example. Do you notice any tightness in those areas? Are you holding 'stuff' in or holding 'stuff' out?

We use our bodies to display to the outside world how we are doing inside. Whether you acknowledge it or not, it is this way. Modern communication technology states that our body language communicates much of our messages to people. Ever wonder what your body is saying to others that you do not even notice?

Your emotions are also a huge player in your internal world. How expressive are you with your emotions? Do you fully get them across to others in a respectful way, both respecting yourself and them? Do you minimize your feelings and present a show for others? Do you imagine what others may think of you before you express yourself emotionally? Do you hold back because of embarrassment or shame?

Emotions are the connective material, the juice that links you to others—kind of an energetic highway. The way you present your emotions reflects the amount of trust you have in yourself and the relationships around you. If your trust level is low there is no way on earth you will show up emotionally as you really are.

It is good practice to notice how you present yourself emotionally to others. Are you minimizing the emotion, taking the edge off? Or are you adding to the emotion to make it more dramatic? Either action is a statement of your emotional health. You know if you are holding back or making more of something.

Your emotions are just what they are in each moment. There is no good or bad about them, no right or wrong. They are just emotions, energy in motion as Bradshaw has so correctly put it. The way to work with your emotions is to start to notice them; notice them internally and see whether you are presenting them exactly as they are. There will be a gap between the internal emotion and its expression out in the world. Aim for the place where internal emotions and external expression are identical, no withholding, no embellishing. Anything else is a function of an imbalance of the other three quadrants in your internal self. Track down the imbalance; then work to bring full balance to your inner self.

Your spirit is the dynamic most difficult to explain. Most of us settle for the esoteric notion of some sort of Godhead or Divine being that is an ideal outside of ourselves. Few of us ever allow the Truth of our Divinity to be just that. It is a sense of self that is beyond the body, mind, and emotions.

A sense of always having been and always will be. It is a sense of being bigger than our own lives, a feeling of out-living ourselves.

Being in touch with your spiritual depth through meditation, daily yoga practice, prayer or genuine caring, truly supports your whole self. This part of you is the one that in my opinion is most often left behind. It's discounting creates a spiritual hole in your being that you often try to replace by relying on the other three dynamics. You try to eat yourself full, sex yourself to completion, distract yourself from the pain you feel. There is in most of you a deep sense of emptiness, something missing. You have the American Dream handled and yet there exists within you this gaping wound, this deep knowing that you are missing something. These are all signs that your spirit has not been well taken care of.

Look for this in yourself. Notice the place where you feel less than complete. Notice what you do to fill yourself up. What manner of mind, body, or emotional tricks do you play in order to get some relief from that deep sense of emptiness? Seriously, notice how you try to fill the hole from the outside. Is it possible? Are you having success doing it that way?

No, of course not.

Perhaps it is time to try something else that will more directly address the emptiness you feel deep within your being.

So that takes care of the internal dynamic, how you do your life from the inside. Now how do you take that internal sense of self and press it into the world?

The outer ring of the model has four distinct components, communication, personal beliefs, risk taking and self-worth. These four elements create a dynamic through which our inner world gets translated into the outer world. Again, as in the inner self dynamic, these elements are interconnected and reinforce each other both in a positive and negative fashion.

For example, if I have a low sense of self worth, my willingness to take risks, to communicate with others and to push through my personal beliefs will be understandably low. I will likely not speak my needs clearly nor really tell it like it is. I will hide my realness behind some sort of mask.

Do you get how it is all linked?

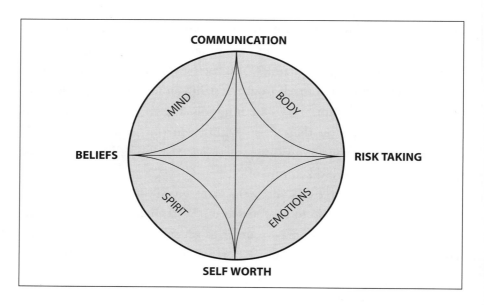

Communication in this model is simply you getting yourself across to others in a way that they can understand. You would use all communication channels and present mind, body, emotional, and spiritual aspects fully with no add-ons or take-aways. No filters so to speak. It would be just you speaking directly to someone else with no manipulation, no distractions, no ulterior motives, just pure and direct communication.

Personal beliefs are those mental models you have built in order to protect yourself from further damage. You create them as a result of events that often brought you pain and hurt when you were younger. The beliefs you create about yourself become fixed and rigid over time, so much so that you think these 'rules' are really you, valid to the core. The fable Rip Van Winkel speaks to the nature of these beliefs…falling asleep in our lives…

going on autopilot and allowing the belief system to run the show as we sleep in absentia somewhere deep behind the scene.

These beliefs are filters through which data going out and data coming in get translated. One such belief could be "I am not good enough." How this nasty filter works is something like this. Someone pays you a compliment, something about how good a job you did. Even before the compliment is complete your mind will kick in and find ways to discount the communication. Things like, "Oh well, it was the best I could do." "But can't you see the mess I made on one thing or another." Either way the compliment will be headed off at the pass and not allowed to enter your inner domain. You will fight it to the death because it goes against your personal belief structure.

The power of this belief structure is awesome. It holds millions of people back from living from their real depth, from their real light, from their real magic.

Risk taking is the third element of the outer circle and it too plays a significant role in how we relate to the outside world. It is a simple concept to grasp. It is your willingness to just do it. To just say it, be it, hear it, feel it, smell it and taste it.

Just the way it is.

It is being on that edge of your life where it feels oh so real and vital. It can look like reckless abandon. Your willingness to risk it has a direct impact on how you show up in your own life. How authentic you are and how much of your personal power you are willing to own.

For me, in this context, risk taking has an opposite—blame. Blame is pinning your life on the actions of others; pointing fingers and finding fault everywhere except where you have influence—your own life. So watch for this one in your own speaking, and listen to where you place power in your sentences and paragraphs. Are you giving away your power by blaming others? Or do you own your power by making responsible personal statements, and by taking a risk by showing up as you actually are.

Here is an example. "You really piss me off you flirt." This statement puts the blame squarely on the shoulders of the other person. It is like pointing a finger at someone using words. By using the word "you," full responsibility for your emotional state has been given to the other. Here is a more responsible way to say the same thing. "I feel really angry when I see you hugging other guys."

Lastly, the much talked about category **self worth**. Others call it self esteem. I prefer the phrase self worth because it speaks directly to personal value. This gem is a challenging one, the one that is the subtle undermining influence in your ability to relate to the outside world. Many of you suffer from a chronic lack of self-worth. You have had it beaten out of you over the years. Some of you may look confident but when you get below the veneer and check out the hard wood it is not so confident.

In simple terms it is how you feel about yourself at the core. Am I good enough in my own estimation or not? Self worth is personal, subjective, and there is little anyone outside yourselves can do for you to increase your sense of self worth. It is a personal struggle and requires regular attention. You can spot low self worth easily. Comments like; "oh it was nothing." or "I can never get anything right." or "Well it looks easy but I am sure to mess it up." All these are phrases that people with low self worth regularly use.

Low self worth keeps you small. Unhealthy or fake self worth gets you in over your head and sets you up for failure that will further increase your sense of not being good enough. Healthy self worth is a solid sense of knowing who and what you are, what you are capable of and what you can really accomplish in the world. Look for how you keep yourself small or conversely how you take on the unachievable. Both are a sign of low self worth.

How to increase your sense of self worth…treat yourself well when you accomplish things in your life. Give your own self a pat on the back when you deserve it.

So that does it, the Personal Spiritual Growth Wheel in a nutshell. There will be further conversations about it at the end of each chapter.

The Growth Spiral

This tool is basically a reminder tool. Its sole purpose is to graphically show you how personal growth evolves, the path it could travel. It demystifies the notion of ever being finished with your personal growth. It debunks the Myth of Perfection.

Most of you believe that if you just do enough weekend workshops, enough therapy sessions that some day sooner or later you will be done.

Not true.

Though you may make progress and do some excellent clearing work, it simply never gets done. Somewhere in your mind-body will always be the remnants of your past. You will never be completely over Mom, Dad, and your fear of being alone.

The Growth Spiral demonstrates two key factors. *(See figure next page)*

Personal growth does not occur in a straight line but is more like a roller coaster. You make some gains and get a clear view of what lies beyond. You cascade into the depths of an unexpected valley and see nothing but the pit. You rise and fall almost continually along your journey.

Secondly the spiral shows you that you will over time keep tripping over some of the more major issues in your life. The more recent, less traumatic events may even be cleared from your universe. However those people, places, and events that left you deeply hurt, betrayed or traumatized will likely keep recurring at deeper and deeper levels of unconsciousness. In other words, you will never be done!

You will always have issues in your life. You may have made great progress around your Dad issues, however some time down the therapy road, or the workshop highway Dad pops up again for yet another look see.

This is how it has been in my life over the past 17 years and I am far from an unusual guy, as a matter of fact I am quite ordinary. So it is easy for me to draw a conclusion that if it was so for me it must be so for all the other ordinary guys out in the real world.

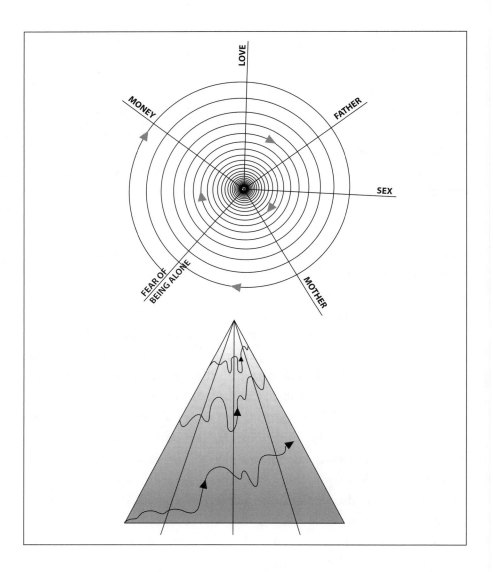

To summarize, yep you do make progress in your personal growth. Yes you do get clear on many issues. Those deeper, historical events will never go away they are in your cells. Though you may gain mastery over them don't expect to ever have them completed.

Reactivity and Criticalness as Personal Growth Tools

Many current writers use the analogy of others as a mirror in which you can see yourself and I have found this to be true. It begs the questions though, how do I make use of the mirror? And how can I see myself reflected in another?

Well I stumbled across a few helpful hints over the years. Two in particular have helped me immensely…reactivity and criticalness.

Let me explain.

Criticalness, at least when I find myself critical, usually speaks to things that I have personally done and not taken responsibility for. Here is an example from my life. I recall a time when I was super critical of a guy driving drunk, I was really criticizing him to a friend I was driving with. My pal noticed I was over the top with my berating of this fellow and said so. He was right. As I looked at my criticalness I recalled several times in my life when I was so plastered I shouldn't have even walked home, yet I hopped in my car and drove. I never owned up to that, never spoke of how shitty I felt, how much guilt I had around it. I could have killed somebody and I knew it.

You see what was going on?

I was speaking to this other drunk driver as I really wanted to speak to myself. I really wanted someone to call me on my personal irresponsibility for driving when I knew I should have taken a cab. My criticalness, in this case, encouraged me to come clean with my friend and confess what I had done that was similar.

Watch for criticalness and check to see where you have done a similar thing. Then confess!

Reactivity is much the same type of thing. Ever been in a meeting, a gathering, or party and someone walks into the space and your skin starts to crawl? You are not sure why but for some reason this person really bugs you. They may not have even spoken, or when they speak it may be even worse.

Your tendency is to make it about **them**, put them down in your minds or even openly. You may even call them names. Mostly it is a deep energetic reaction. You want them to leave or you feel the need to leave.

Check your reaction out. What is it in you that they have touched on? What personal button have they pushed? Pointing fingers at them and blaming them for your own reactions will get you nowhere fast. You are simply giving them power over you. Leave them out of it, look inside and notice what is going on for you. Any comments you have should always be a personal reflection of where you are at not a reactive judgment of another.

Using both these two simple tools seems easy. It is—simply practice looking in at yourself and taking responsibility for your own universe. There is usually much more work to do on yourself than you can get done in a lifetime. So it is best to do your own personal work and thank the others for highlighting areas where you may need to concentrate.

Positive and Negative Indicators

Positive and negative indicators are much like road signs for a personal journey. It is simple. A negative indicator says stop. A positive indicator says continue along, albeit watchfully looking for the next indicator.

If you are in a job for example and you start sleeping in and being late or if you start to phone in sick more often and you begin to feel a building resentment towards your fellow employees there may be something there for you to look into. These indicators are saying to you that something is not well in your work life, something is out. It demands some personal intro-spection, a real good look at what you are doing and how your are spending your life energy.

It may be that you are unable to relate well to your co-workers. You may have unspoken messages for other employees. You may be in some sort of power struggle with your boss. Your salary may be too low in your

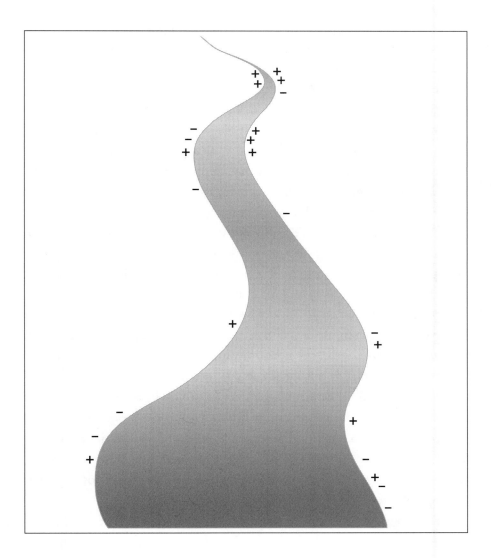

estimation. Who knows? When you are getting negative indicators such as these you need to look into the cause or you are destined to end up in an ugly emotional kind of dead zone where you simply are putting in time. In a way you have actually quit your job without leaving. What a way to spend your life!

Negative indicators also apply to our personal relationships. We see it all the time. We battle with each other often. Conflict is common and the battle of the sexes, the war between parent and child goes on. There are negative signs along the way we can watch for, signs that would point out we are off track. Not making eye contact, not telling the truth, avoiding contact, bad or no sex, little or no hugging or physical contact, a lack of humour and laughter. All are signs that things in our relationships are not well. Usually we ignore them hoping things will get better. But things don't get better, and we still tend to ignore the signs until it is too late.

Use negative indicators as stop signs. Stop, look and listen to what is happening in the environment in which you are picking up these negative sign posts. Take a real look at what is going on in your life and notice the negatives, learn from them and make different choices.

Positive indicators will likely not be as glaring as the negatives. You should however, begin to sense a deeper more rested level of happiness in your life. As a man you will likely feel more on your edge, more challenged and more satisfied. You will likely not spend too much time with distractions like television, over-drinking, or mental gymnastics. You will notice you are more present in your life, for your woman, family, friends and work colleagues.

You should also notice an increase in your cash flow and net worth over time. A fuller sex life and more attraction to feminine things is another positive indicator. You should feel more radiance and love flowing from your woman.

These positive indicators encourage us as men to continue moving forward. And yes we need to keep a watchful eye open for more sign posts along the way. As we continue to grow and evolve as men so do our needs to live from a deeper purpose, to live more fully sharing our personal strengths, and our personal dreams. This is how men leave a legacy for their children.

Watch for both negative and positive indicators let them point the way.

1
And So It Begins
Jody's Death is the Beginning of My Life

The Story As I Remember It

Judging by North American standards I had my life pretty much together. I was living in downtown Toronto in a three-story brownstone apartment. As an employee of one of Canada's premier investment firms I was paid a good six-figure salary. I was a member of a downtown squash club. I played golf, commercial league hockey and ran marathons. I volunteered my time to two worthy causes, and had a beautiful fiancé; Brigit was studying to become massage therapist. We went on wonderful vacations, enjoyed the benefits of the good life, tickets to the arts, sports, and evenings of dining and celebrating with good friends. Within reason we had everything we wanted and then some. Life was good.

I was living the American Dream.

I was a success. Or so it seemed.

It was a Friday evening; we had just got in from a night on the town. The telephone was ringing off the hook. Part of me wanted to ignore the damn thing and hop into bed with my fiancé; another part of me felt a sense of urgency in the ring, an insistence that for some reason I could not ignore.

"Hello" I said.

"Hi, it's Roy, Jody is gone" he blurted out.

Jody was my sister. She and her husband Roy lived in Ste. Catherine's, Ontario outside of Toronto, a wee bit beyond Hamilton. Roy wasn't much of a fellow for words and seldom spoke on the telephone.

"Where has she gone?" I asked, thinking she had left for an unexpected trip.

"She is just gone!" Roy repeated. As my head began to clear and I focused more on how Roy was speaking. I realized by the tone in his voice that all was not well.

"Roy, what's up man, where has she gone? What's going on?" I questioned.

Roy was unable to carry on with our conversation and before I knew it he had passed the telephone over to his Mom. Things started to feel even worse as I listened to her emotion-filled voice explain the happenings of earlier in the evening.

Jody had been helping a friend move. The job was done and she felt tired and mentioned to her friends that she was going to lie down and take a short nap on the couch. She did. A short time later her friends checked in on her and found her dead. She had died of a soft tissue brain aneurysm.

Roy had been calling me since 6:30 pm. It was now near midnight.

I was stunned.

All I could think of asking was, "Do my parents know?"

"No, Stephen we thought it was best for such awful news to come from you. Could you handle telling your folks?" Roy's Mom asked.

"Yes. We'll call you tomorrow and make plans for the funeral I guess," was all I could muster.

I hung the telephone up and looked at Brigit. A few tears ran down my face and I had a quick cry as I related the news to her. I quickly pulled myself together and began figuring out what to do next. No way could I call my folks on the telephone and give them the news; we needed to make the 30-minute trip up the Don Valley Parkway to Scarborough and deliver the message in person.

By the time we pulled into the driveway it must have been close to 1:00 am. The highway was empty and the suburbs were quiet, not many lights on and only a few homes shining with the glow of late night television.

I rang the doorbell.

It seemed like forever before Dad opened the door; time was doing weird things since the news. I was a bit shocked to see him carrying a baseball bat in his hand—a sign of the times I guess.

"Dad we need to come in". I said as firmly and stoically as I could. "Have a seat Dad I have some really bad news to share." Dad had barely got his bottom on the chair in the living room when I blurted, "Jody's dead. She died earlier tonight from a blood clot in her brain. Roy was unable to call so here I am".

Poor Dad was overcome by the news and muttered, "Oh God not poor Jody." He kept a close reign on his emotions. The three of us sat silently in the living room for what seemed an eternity, it was likely only a minute or two before I offered,

"I think we should head upstairs and tell Mom".

We did.

The four of us sat around the bed stunned, lost in a conversation about when it would be best to call the rest of the family, my sister Sue in Nova Scotia, my brother Peter in the Yukon, and sister Carrie just north of Toronto. At my insistence the calls were made right then and there. Sue had a feeling about it and had been awake for an hour or so. Peter began planning his trip from the Yukon. Carrie couldn't believe her ears.

The news was out…Jody was dead.

The next day and the following days were a blur. Too many new names, faces, arrangements, funeral parlor, family, emotions, endless gatherings created a deep sense of confusion in me. Something was not right here and I couldn't put my finger on it. Some weird things began happening inside me, weird only because I had never felt or thought in these ways before. My emotions were all stirred up and I began having chats with God. I hadn't prayed or acknowledged God since I was in my early teens. Now for some reason God popped up and I was engaging in weird little chats with him. Looking for an answer I guess.

Out of all the goings on around Jody's death I remember three things very clearly. How many friends she had, really good friends that I didn't even know; she had a life I knew little or nothing about; and, I recall the deep sense of guilt I was carrying—I was alive and Jody was not.

The first memory I have is just how many people loved Jody.

That first Saturday when the Garrett family arrived at the Baker home in St. Catherines (Jody's in-laws) was quite a scene. Cars everywhere, the house packed, people chatting everywhere in the Baker home; the driveway and front yard, the front porch, the kitchen packed, as was the living room and family room. People I had never met before were chatting about Jody, their memories of her and the sense of loss they were feeling. The funeral parlour was no different—people from all over the place filled the rooms for the entire day and evening; all of them reminiscing about their friend, my sister Jody.

I remember the church on the day Jody was buried. As I lifted the coffin off the stand and moved toward the centre isle, I looked up and noticed a sea of faces. The church was absolutely packed, as was the entranceway. As the procession moved through the hall to the front door and towards the steps I noticed people lined up on the steps down the sidewalk and into the parking lot. There were hundreds and hundreds of people; some faces I knew, many more I did not.

I remember being in awe of the number of people my sister had in her life, a life I knew very little about.

The second memory is of a conversation I had with God.

We had left the funeral parlour after a planning session the day before the funeral and were on our way to Jody's house to pick out some clothes for her to wear and a few precious things to put in the coffin with her. Roy, Mom, sister Sue, Brigit and I were there, perhaps Peter too. I remember being in Jody's bedroom looking through her supply of wild and crazy clothes, her trademark, thinking what I would like to see her in. I was overcome by a deep sense of sadness and bolted from the house. I ran to the end of the street and found my way down a path to a secluded point overlooking the water. I sat and cried like a child for the first time since Jody's death, the first time in decades.

As the crying passed I found myself in a conversation with God. Actually it was more like a sales pitch. I wanted Jody back alive and I was negotiating with God for her safe return. Knowing only God could hit a one-iron I offered up my set of Ping golf clubs, no deal. I offered my sporty Ford Merkur XR4TI...nope. My RRSPs and all my bank deposits...still not a nibble. My job, my music collection and all my stuff, "Take it all!" I begged and began weeping deeply again. Through the sobbing I offered myself.

"Take me you fucking prick, take me!! Just give Jody back her life!!" I wailed.

There was no deal making today.

God was not in the mood for any such negotiations. "Your sister Jody is dead Stephen. Accept that fact, face it, deal with it and get on with living. There is nothing you can offer Me, nothing you can do for Me. She is dead and you are alive."

It felt so final, and I felt so helpless.

Finally, the guilt.

I guess it is called survivor's guilt in the hospice field; doesn't matter much what it is called. I was feeling extremely guilty for being alive. I just couldn't put it together. None of it made sense.

I was a party animal, money focused and selfish. Living the American Dream and not really giving a shit about much other than myself. Jody was this wonderful, authentic, creative, spiritual and community focused woman who just seemed to care about people. Why would God make this choice? Leave a shit like me behind and take an amazing woman like Jody. Only the good die young, a line in a Billy Joel song coursed through my mind. None of it made sense to me and I felt guilty as hell for being alive.

What was worse, I felt guilty that Jody died without knowing how much I loved her.

In the Moment

The whole experience didn't make any sense to me. I was an emotional basket case, confused about life, uncertain about my personal beliefs, and emotionally shaken. Everything I thought I could rely on was now very much in question. I was in deep personal crisis and didn't even know it. I handled it the way I had always handled difficult things; I shut down. I had no idea what to do or what to think, it was all very foreign to me, I was looking for the simplest way just to survive. So I did what I was taught to do. I kept a stiff upper lip. Imagine that. Lowering my sister's body into the ground, into her grave, and struggling to hold it together when all I really felt like doing was holding her close to my body and crying deeply for her death. Fuck!

What I Did with It Then

I was frightened and felt very lost and alone. Although I had been able to handle life's ups and downs, I was now in a place where I needed outside help; thankfully I had the blind courage to reach out. Six months after Jody's death I found a Men's group that ultimately led me to personal spiritual therapist. Though I struggled like hell with the idea of going for help, it was the best thing I could have done even though it went against all my beliefs and my thoughts that it was a sign of weakness and failure for men to reach out for support.

I was taught real men don't eat quiche—real men tough it out, don't need help and lord knows must always appear strong.

How I Think and Feel About It Now

I have missed Jody since the day of her death yet I am grateful for her passing. Her death was the catalyst for my own awakening; it was the kick start I needed to get off my comfortable ass and dive deeply into what was real and meaningful in my life. It was the push I needed to embrace my own spirituality; to take the first step back on to my spiritual path and take full responsibility for my life. It was Jody's death that breathed life back into me. I realize now that I do my best 'learning', and grow the most as a human being when I am in a crisis or situation of deep personal loss.

Using the Personal Growth Wheel, internally I was in need of some emotional work and professional support; externally my beliefs were getting in my way of moving forward through my sister's death. I needed to address both these quadrants if I were to be able to get on with my life and not stay mentally and emotionally stuck. Using outside help, in this case personal therapy, I was able to over time express fully my grief and my guilt. I was also able to have a close look at the beliefs I had lived my life by up to this point. Slowly I was able to begin changing some of my patterns.

What I Would Do Differently

The two changes I would make if I had the opportunity to do it again would be these:

I would find a way to express my love for my sister, any way, just to let her know that I loved and cared for her. It could be a telephone call, mailing her a card, sending her a flower, or simply saying "I love you" to her in person.

I would not hold back my grief and sadness. I would do my best to let my emotions out, to express myself authentically in the moment.

Notes to the Regular Guy's Handbook

1) Death is more often an opening, an opportunity, as opposed to a door closing. Embracing death, particularly one's own death, is the key to living life to its fullest. As a man, feel deeply your own death, you only have so much time to leave your legacy.

2) Asking for help and support is a sign of courage and wisdom; not a sign of weakness and failure.

2

The Foundation is Crumbling
My Journey Begins

The Story As I Remember It

There is an old expression that time heals all. What a bunch of shit that is!

Though the days and weeks rolled on, a deep sense of confusion, the raw emotions, and an intense desire to figure this thing called life out were ever present for me. No matter how I tried to distract myself, this hunger to know never went away. Ever! It gnawed away at me endlessly, especially the desire to find out what life was really about. Though it looked on the surface that all was well with me, that I was getting through the loss and moving on with my life, it was all an act.

I was floundering and needed help. I just didn't know where to look or what to look for.

Oddly enough my fiancé Brigit had been encouraging me to take The Sterling Men's Weekend. Like a typical alpha male I would have nothing to do with that kind of touchy feely group stuff, and quickly dismissed the idea. Brigit though, stayed with it and three weeks after Jody's death reminded me of an open-house I had promised (in a dismissive way) to attend. Though I tried to get out of it, in the end I tagged along.

Well it was horrible.

Approximately 200 people showed up to hear this Sterling guy give us his sales pitch. What was worse, the organizers had the guys sit on one side of the hall and the gals on the other. I found myself in a weird environment I really didn't want to be in, surrounded by a bunch of men I could care less about. All I could think of was trying to find an inconspicuous way to escape without losing face with Brigit.

Just as I had created my escape route Justin Sterling, the leader of The Sterling Institute of Relationship, strolled onto the floor. I was fucked; couldn't leave now the big guy was on stage delivering his presentation.

I don't remember much about what he said. Some stuff made sense intuitively; other stuff just pissed me off. I guess he spoke for about 45 minutes and then with the force of a monsoon wind the men were swept into one enrollment room and the women were organized in another.

The sales pitch and that awful manipulative style of enrollment filled the room. Being a salesman myself I could feel it coming. All the goading: Where is your commitment? Aren't you worth it? Don't you want to be the man you always wanted to be? Finger pointing, centering men out, all that stuff, I hated it! The more I hated it the more it went on, and on, and on. I couldn't stand it any longer! I stood up abruptly and headed for the exit door.

Some fellow named Doug, sitting at the enrollment desk, asked in a surprisingly gentle manner if I would be signing up. As he asked the question he carefully pushed an enrollment card my way and said, "Its only $450.00. It'll be the best money you've ever spent."

I moved closer to the table and before I knew it I signed up for the June 18–19, 1988 Men's Weekend in New York City! I had no idea why.

As I left the room for the front entrance hall I began to realize I had no sense of what I was getting myself into. All of a sudden I was scared shitless. My God, I'd be in New York City in two weeks with two hundred men doing some sort of group thing all in the same place at the same time with no women. It seemed like a totally crazy thing to do.

It was so different from anything I had ever done before. It was way out of my personal comfort zone, yet somewhere in my body for some reason I knew it was the right thing for me to do.

I made my way to the entrance hall and bumped right into Brigit. I was so preoccupied with what I had just committed to do that I wasn't paying much attention.

"Well?" she asked.

"Well, I'm going to New York in two weeks. I've signed up for the damn weekend." I confessed. Brigit looked radiantly happy.

In the Moment

I was scared out of my wits. I had never done any personal growth work in my life. I was a private fellow and kept most everything to myself. I didn't particularly trust men and in fact I really didn't like most of them much. Yet I was heading to New York to do this weekend workshop with two hundred plus guys I had never met.

I was so frightened over the next days that I could hardly sleep, work, or keep up with my daily routine. In my head I badly wanted to find a way out of going, yet each time I was given an opportunity to back out I simply continued to move ahead with the plans. It was the craziest thing I had ever done in my life and yet I knew I was going. Something larger than me seemed to be in charge of my life.

What I Did with It Then

I kept my word. My father and grandfather had taught me the importance of keeping my word, so I did just that. I faced the fear, felt it, and just kept heading for New York City.

How I Think And Feel About It Now

Truth works in magical ways, and usually when I least expect it. My intuition, if I pay attention, will always lead me in the right direction. My mind on the other hand usually tries to talk me out of paying attention to what I am intuitively sensing I need to do. For some reason, though my mind chatter was unbearably loud, I followed my gut feeling. It was step two towards my own self-discovery. It was absolutely the best thing I could have done for myself. I have learned that leaning into my fear a bit and going ahead anyway is good to do more often than not. It brought me to my edge, a place I know I need to be regularly in my life.

Using the Personal Growth Wheel as a model, you can notice that I was working internally on my spirit. For far too long I had neglected taking good care of myself spiritually and the pull I felt was some sort of internal balancing that was most necessary for me. The outer quadrant was all about taking risks, challenging my existing belief system and going ahead at any rate. My low self esteem, personal beliefs and communication style all leaned against the Men's Weekend. However, I was able to risk it somehow. It was a blind roll of the dice, a total risk.

I was also noticing that even though I was scared to death, I felt more alive in my life than I had for years, and that my squash game also improved. Positive indicators!

What I Would Do Differently

In this situation, nothing. I did what I had to do to get 'growing' in my life, to regain some of my lost personal power and passion.

Notes to the Regular Guy's Handbook

3) The teacher shows up when the student is ready.
4) Trust your deepest calling in each moment and follow it.

3
Me, New York, and a Bunch of Men
Spiritual Baby Steps

The Story As I Remember It

I must admit the Sterling Men's Division did an excellent job of handling the logistics of getting us men to New York. Rides to the airport were organized, and the flight was booked, as was the bus trip to the Days Inn Hotel. The rooms were booked and room assignments were in place at check in. All I had to do was show up; and that I did.

There were about 15 men hanging around the Toronto Island Municipal Airport, all of us assuming that the other men were also heading off to the slaughter. Nobody asked though, and the atmosphere remained silent and awkward. It felt a bit like sitting on the bench waiting for the school principal to send me home with a suspension notice.

The flight and subsequent bus ride went off without a hitch and I all of a sudden found myself in the lobby of the Days Inn in New York City. I checked in, and claimed my bed in a room shared by men who I would soon meet. My nervous energy was palpable. I could barely stay in my skin never mind stay still alone in a strange hotel room.

Off to the lobby I went.

I met up with an actor fellow from Toronto who was also there to do the men's weekend so we both, glad for the distraction, trundled off for dinner at a sushi restaurant. We chatted rather mindlessly, both of us glad to pass the time. I was so preoccupied with wild thoughts about the weekend, nervous anticipation, and a huge dose of fear that I remember little of the conversation we had. I can't even recall the fellow's name.

Dinner was over and we both walked quietly back to the hotel.

There were two other guys in my room, both from Toronto. I was so fucking scared my mind was not functioning at all. Small details escaped me in the moment and still escape me all these years later. I think we chatted for a while and then we all tucked in for a sleepless night.

The alarm rang.

We all got up and readied for the day. A quick breakfast in the hotel dining room with a few more of the lads and we headed off to the Sterling Men's Weekend. As we got closer to the workshop site more and more men were joining in the walk; it soon looked like a parade. We turned the corner towards the school and the line up to get into the workshop loomed huge in front of us. There was lots of noise towards the rear of the line up. Moving closer and closer to the entrance though, the men became more and more subdued. Once inside the school building, only feet from the check-in desk, the silence became deafening.

We were put through some sort of check-in routine and then passed to a guide who took us to an auditorium where we were all to wait for our next instructions. Though some of the guys seemed loud and boisterous the tone in the room was one of nervousness and abject fear. We were next shuffled off to the gym where the workshop was to take place and to my surprise there were women operating the video equipment and handling some duties at what looked like a control table at the back of the gym.

For a while we all sat there and waited. As time went on though some of the guys became impatient; they started giving the women a hard time and raising hell in their own ways. After an hour or so of this I was becoming very impatient and beginning to resent the fact that I had paid good money for this workshop but I was simply sitting around waiting for this Sterling fellow to show up.

As I did at the introductory evening I began to plan my escape; while planning away, however, I noticed men were gradually replacing the women at various posts throughout the gymnasium. As the last woman left her post after being replaced by a man, I got the sense we were about to begin. Many of the men by now were acting out, goofing around and behaving like a bunch of schoolboys bored out of their minds. As the mayhem intensified and reached a crescendo a voice could be heard over the racket of the men. Our weekend had just begun!

Justin spoke.

I have no idea what he said and my recollection of the weekend's details are poor. I know there was an opening talk by Justin and he laid out how the workshop would go. He introduced his staff and gave some examples of the exercises we would be doing. I know we did many exercises, had meals and breaks, it was all a blur to me though. I do remember the anger work, the ceremonial dancing, the sex talk, the cigars, the dark, and the father work.

It was a typical build-up break through weekend formula, and you know what it worked! I won't go into all the details. I will share with you, though, two peak experiences I had: the anger work and the final celebration. They were the pivotal moments in this my first effort towards personal spiritual growth.

It was the last exercise of the first day, well into the night or more likely early morning. We were instructed to make a mental list of the women we were angry at in our lives. Easy task I thought and began developing my list, ex-wife, several ex-girlfriends, a couple of gals who had refused me, my Mom, and oh yeah my sister Susan.

The next instruction was to find a partner and set up in a dyad (*dyo* is Greek for two). We would take turns, one man would express his anger toward a woman or women he was angry at, the other man listening and receiving. After 10 minutes a change over signal would be given and the roles would switch. The listening partner would rant and the fellow who just ranted would listen. I chose to listen first, as I was actually way too frightened to let go of my anger. I had been well taught to control myself and never express anger—one of those modern day family things. I don't remember much of what my partner did, but he sure got at it. Man, he was one angry fellow. Good thing I have my shit together, I thought smugly to myself. Before I knew it the change over call was made.

Now I was face to face with my anger.

One thing I had done throughout the weekend was to throw myself 100% into each exercise. I made a choice as the weekend began that I was going to participate full on and I had done so with each and every exercise. The fear of expressing my anger wasn't going to stop me.

So I began.

I started with my ex-wife and did some surface yelling, some name-calling and you know it began to feel good. It was nice to get some of that stuff out, really nice in fact. So I kept going, and going.

"You fucking cunt…how could you screw around with those guys. You cock sucking bitch, you fucking whore. I hate your fucking guts you slimy fucking douche bag!!!!!" I was angry, I hadn't realized how much anger I had stuffed down over the years. "Fuck you!!!" I bellowed, spit and saliva spewed from my mouth, sweat pouring from my brow.

Then without a moment's notice my anger was being leveled at my recently deceased sister Jody.

"Fuck you Jody, how dare you fucking die without saying goodbye, you fucking bitch!"

"Don't you realize how much I loved you, how fucking dare you die just like that!"

"You get your sorry fucking ass back here you bitch!"

" Fuck you Jody you fucking' quitter, you fucking wimp, I hate your fucking guts for dying…fuck you…Fuck You…FUCK YOU…FUCK YOU…FUCK YOU…FUCK YOU…"

A bell rang or someone whistled to end the anger portion of our work.

The first day of my Men's Weekend was done.

I was numb and dumbfounded, there were some men still hanging around the gym as I came back to my senses. I left quietly, deep in some sort of meditative state. My anger towards Jody had caught me totally by surprise. I don't remember thinking as I walked back to the hotel. I felt a bit like a zombie meandering emptily along the sidewalks. I entered my hotel room unaware of any of the others and went to bed.

Sunday morning came quickly and before I knew it I was walking back to the workshop site with some of the other fellows. We filed into the gym, watched a few of the 'lates' get consequences. Then, the day began. It was a full on day just like Saturday was. Another set of exercises designed to continue the process of building up the energy, preparing us for a peak breakthrough. It built and built all day; through lunch and supper right into the late evening, right up to the point of the final exercise.

We formed a large circle in the gym. The instruction was to either put yourself or a man you would not trust in battle in the centre of the circle. The men you would go into battle with remained in the outside circle. Once the movement into and out of the centre of the circle was complete, those men in the centre were taken 'downstairs'. The outer circle of men was then instructed to create a celebration that would welcome the men from downstairs into the circle of 'men'. It was a form of 'right of passage'.

I was one of the upstairs guys.

I took full advantage of the body paints that were there for our use. Surprising to me I took off all my clothes and painted my body red. I grabbed an African-looking mask and joined the 'dance' some men were taking part in. The music boomed, the room was full of smoke machine fog and began to take on a very tribal feel. Early in the celebration I noticed some of the men hugging the walls and corners; the goings on were just too much for them in that moment I guess even though they were selected as warriors.

Somewhere along the way I fell into a deep trance-like state and simply became the 'warrior dancer'. I danced with an abandon I hadn't felt in years. I was all at once lost in the moment yet more present than I had ever been in my adult life. I danced and celebrated from the depths of my masculine heart and soul.

The men from downstairs were gradually ushered into the celebration and before I knew it we were all together again in joyous leaping and jumping. It was an amazing event. So tribal. So masculine. So alive, and yet so unreal.

I was simply blown away.

In seemingly a moment's notice it all somehow came to an end. I recall looking around for my clothes and struggling to get dressed. I was a red, sweaty hunk of man. We circled up and were instructed to work our way towards Justin and say or do what ever came up as a way of thanks. In the moment I was so open and so vulnerable and in such an altered state I thought Justin was some type of God.

I said my good-byes to him, bowed, and left for the hotel.

I must have looked pretty scary to folks. It was the wee hours of Monday morning and I was walking through downtown New York painted red, with red stains all over my clothes and in my hair. I found a grocery store along the way and bought a couple of bottles of coke and continued on my way to the Days Inn, wondering all the way why the guy at the counter had looked at me with such a weird glance. When I saw myself in the mirror in the bathroom of my hotel room I knew why!

I hopped into the shower to wash up. My body was full of energy. I was totally alive and felt everything with a new sense of awareness. It was like I was in a new body, so vital and so vibrant. I couldn't bear the huge energy that was coursing through every cell in my body. I hadn't felt so alive, so sensual, so horny in years! The next moment I had grabbed my erect cock and began masturbating. When I ejaculated it nearly knocked me off my feet; I had never experienced such fullness of energy and such a huge release in my life!

I stumbled into bed fully spent, happy to be a man, and grateful to be alive.

In the Moment

I had no idea what had happened. Yeah sure I was at this men's weekend, but what the hell had shifted in me? What had gone on? Who was this Justin Sterling guy? Mostly though, I was concerned about how I was going to share my experience with Brigit. I was so blasted open that I didn't even realize it in the moment. I thought I was normal, my old self.

All in all I was feeling much better than ever before but wasn't really sure why in the moment, though it is easy in hindsight to figure it out.

What I Did with It Then

I made the mistake many seekers of Truth make. I attributed all my growth to a charismatic leader, in this case, Justin Sterling; I put him up on a pedestal and became a full on Sterling Men's Division groupie. I took no credit for my own breakthrough. I gave of myself to the Sterling Men's Division because I thought it was them who had 'saved' my sorry life. I became an active participant of a cult and didn't even know it.

How I Think and Feel About It Now

How I see it now…The Sterling Men's Weekend was a beginning for me in my personal spiritual growth. It was my first step and it was full of dead ends, potholes and challenges. I had never done any personal growth work before. I had no idea about how to do it, what the exercises were about or how I should feel and think. It was like learning a new language. All the uncertainty and confusion aside, it got me on my way and I am eternally grateful to Justin for the lessons I learned at his workshop.

By the way I no longer hold Justin as some type of God; he is just a guy like me who had the courage to give his gift fully to the world. He is as human as am I, and he too puts his pants on one leg at a time. In that moment he was the teacher I needed; it was perfect. Now he is a man like me with his strengths and weaknesses, just like me.

What was going on in my personal growth was clear. In my external world I had just spent a weekend communicating more fully with others about my real life, I had improved my communication skills and along with it I experienced a lift in my sense of self-worth. My personal belief system lost some of its grip on me and I was more willing to take greater risks. These were all positive indicators and a reflection of how the dynamics of the external ring of the Personal Spiritual Growth Wheel work.

Internally I had spent some good time clearing out some of my emotional baggage, bringing my inner world into better balance. The tribal celebration also addressed my need for ritual in my life. I somehow felt closer to God, so I was taking good care of my inner world. I felt more alive in my body than I had for years, since I was a teenager in fact!

What I Would Do Differently

I would not give my personal power away to a charismatic leader like Justin Sterling. I would be grateful for the teaching and would remember to give thanks to the Great One. I would also celebrate my own efforts and my own growth experience, because after all it was me who did the work! I would acknowledge the guru in me.

Notes to Regular Guy's Handbook

5)   Be grateful for your teachers without giving your power away.

6)   In everything you do, do it 100% full on. It may be the last thing you do before you die.

4
Time to Be Real
Will the Real Stephen Garrett Please Stand Up!

The Story As I Remember It

I was in a real dilemma; I had no idea how to share my adventure with Brigit. I would be face to face with her in 10 hours and had not a clue of what I would say or do. Making a plan became my project through breakfast, on the bus ride to JFK airport, on my flight home, and in the car ride back to my Shuter Street apartment.

You see I was a big talker and always found ways to talk myself into and out of situations. I was a salesman, what else was I supposed to do? However, in this moment I knew that my usual 'sales pitch' wasn't going to work for me or for Brigit. How then would I get across to her the amazing events of my 'weekend'?

Well, the first thought in my head was not to speak at all, and as crazy as it seemed at the time, I decided that would be the first piece of my welcome home celebration with her. So if I am not going to talk how will I get myself across to her? What was it I would say in actions and not words? What was it I wanted her to know about me anyway?

What I wanted was for her to see and get me, the man I actually was. Me, the real me, no more, and no less…just me.

As the plane touched down at Toronto's Municipal Airport I had the workings of a fine welcome home celebration for Brigit. I ran down to the St. Lawrence Market and bought fresh cut flowers, lots of them; fresh fruit and vegetables with some excellent cheese; and oh yes, some Swiss chocolate. Not to forget the freshly squeeze orange juice, candles and incense.

I dashed home with my purchases and set about preparing the celebration. I cleaned the house well, washed the bathroom, made the bed, and totally prepared the space. I placed the candles exactly where I wanted them, the flowers too. It all began to take shape. I selected the right music and listened to it carefully as I cut and prepared the fruit and vegetables.

All the while the only thoughts in my mind were about this celebration. It was almost like a meditation.

I wrote two notes, one for the back door, and one for the front. They simply said, "There will be no talking tonight. I will show you what I learned at my weekend. No talking."

It was all set, all perfect.

I showered and decided as I was cleaning my body that the only way to greet Brigit was naked. It just didn't seem right to be clothed. If I was to show her the real me, naked was the way.

So naked I was.

I was ready an hour before she arrived. I'll tell you it was the longest hour I had ever spent. I swung back and forth between taking all the preparations down and just greeting her the old way and staying with my plan. The longer the wait the more I talked myself into and out of the celebration. When I finally resolved to scrap it all there was a knock on the back door...it was her!

Too late now, no going back!

As I opened the door she began chatting, she was so glad to see me, she couldn't help herself. I gently put my hand over her mouth and looked into her eyes with a feeling of deep, deep love. She understood, stepped inside, and we hugged and kissed.

I led her to the bathroom, slowly and lovingly undressed her. I turned the water on and led her into the shower. The candlelight set a calm and loving feeling in the bathroom. I washed her, cleansed her of the toils of her day, and held her close to me under the warmth of the water. The beauty of her was incredible, naked, wet strong, young female body. She was glowing and radiant.

I stepped out of the shower and got the towels ready, I lifted her out of the tub stood her on the bath mat and dried her from head to toe. I wrapped a fresh towel around her and escorted her into the bedroom where a taste feast was waiting for the both of us. The music was just right and candle-light again set a warm and sensual tone in the room.

I fed her vegetables and cheese and then fruit and chocolate. She did nothing for herself, I served her in every way I could. It was almost like dancing; I had to watch her carefully, listen to her breath, and notice every subtle move she made if I were to serve her needs as fully as I could. Vegetables and cheese, with tastes of white wine in between. Grapes, strawberries, blueberries, and melon; each mouthful of fruit followed by a small piece of chocolate. It was all so perfect, so sensual and so right.

Time disappeared.

The music played on.

I kissed her.

We made love in a way I had always wanted to, in a way that I knew almost as if from birth. I touched her the way she had always wanted to be touched but had never spoken out loud. It was like two Gods making love. There was no rush, no point, no urgency. There was openness, sweetness, and love. It was magical and unrepeatable.

In a timeless instant it was all gone, there was nothing, no room, no music, no Brigit, and no me. There just was. It was as if everything vanished and all that was left was my consciousness. It was glorious! There are no words to even come close to describing what I experienced in the never-ending moment. I had never felt so total and complete and yet so empty in my whole life.

I have no idea how long it lasted and don't really care, but when I came back into my body, into the room, into my bed beside Brigit I almost freaked. The energy was so huge I couldn't stay still. It was like I was filling up the whole damn room with me, my essence, and my energy. I grabbed a pair of running shorts and a t-shirt, I groped for my wallet and headed for the door yelling something like, "Its too big, its too big, I gotta' go!"

Out I ran.

In the Moment

I had no real idea what was going on with me. Something inside of my mind, or body, or brain, had transformed and I was struggling to figure out how to live in what seemed a different world. I knew I had to change the way I was with Brigit, and that in some way I need to find new ways to express myself. I was stumped as to how and my mind wanted me to go back to my old ways of relating and being. I was surprised, confused, and scared. I had no road map to steer me through my newly renovated mind. I felt like I was going crazy.

What I Did with It Then

As I planned the celebration I noticed my negative self-talk and struggled like hell with it. It was like a war going on inside of me; what my heart wanted my over developed ego resisted like hell…I ultimately collapsed under the weight of all the mad chatter of my mind and was all set to stop the evening I had planned; thankfully Divine Grace stepped in and won the day. I had no choice, I somehow carried on with my plan.

How I Think And Feel About It Now

Looking back on these profound events I recognize them as life-changing—they were all awakenings, realizations or enlightenment of some kind. They were all the result of my deep longing for God and for Truth. My deep yearning and my willingness to just go ahead, even though my mind was screaming at me to stop, is what brought me fully into these amazing life-altering events.

I learned the power of taking a risk and relating to the world and others from a more real place. The risk taking I had all of a sudden embraced was bringing very positive changes into my life. Even though I had a minimal understanding of what was going on for me spiritually, I felt much more alive in my life.

Internally I notice that the neglected spiritual sector of my life was getting some much needed attention, and as I worked on honouring that part of me the rest of my internal life also started to improve, I was more expressive emotionally, my mind was less confused. I felt more alive in my body. The dynamics of the Personal Spiritual Growth Wheel were working positively for me as I began to restructure both my internal and external ways of being.

What I Would Do Differently

The awakening I experienced at the Men's Weekend in New York and the profound opening I felt that Monday evening were significant turning points in my life. What I would do now is find a spiritual teacher that could guide me through this period of personal growth. I was a damn banker, I had no idea what was going on within me and I needed someone with whom I could work with in these realms of spirit. I was in a kind of spiritual emergency and needed the wise guidance of a good teacher.

Notes to the Regular Guy's Handbook

7) Trust your deepest intuition.

8) As many good men have said before, feel the fear and go ahead anyway.

9) There is such a thing as Divine Grace.

10) Men have all the natural and creative ability to be outstanding lovers.

11) Spiritual Union through sex is real.

5
You've Got to Be Kidding
At the Corner of Queen and George Yet!

The Story As I Remember It

I was in a daze as I stumbled down the stairs out on to Shuter Street. The experience I just had seemed to catapult me into a different reality. I felt almost mindless, as if I was dreaming.

The next thing I recall was I was walking towards St. Lawrence Market; I had a hankering for a huge vanilla ice cream cone! As I was walking along I noticed I had no shoes on. I was carrying an Eaton's bag with a newly purchased answering machine and a Bible. Odd I thought as I didn't recall buying anything nor even being in Eaton's. However, my hunger for ice cream eclipsed my trying to figure out why I had bought these items. I was definitely in an altered state of being.

Minutes later I was happily licking my triple scoop French vanilla ice cream cone, ambling along the alleys and side streets towards Moss Park and home. I was child-like in those moments. There was absolutely nothing on my mind. I was simply walking along in the moment enjoying my ice cream cone. At one point I skipped along whistling, totally satisfied with my life and loving each and every moment of it!

When I stepped off the sidewalk at the corner of George Street and Queen something other-worldly happened. It was as if I had stepped into another dimension. Everything around me had somehow magically come to life! Colors, sounds, smells, textures, all alive and full of energy. Everything was separate, yet connected, part of the whole, including me. I felt like I was in the movie Alice in Wonderland!

I could see the energy in all things and noticed that nothing really ended. Each object seemed to flow into the space around it. The leaves on the trees seemed not to have an edge; they gradually blended into the air around them. They seemed to go from a dense substance, what we see as the leaf, and became less dense towards their outer edges and gradually becoming so 'thin' that they seemed to disappear into the air. The air and the leaf appeared to be one—totally connected.

I could hear the din of the city; the kind of hum that is always there. In that moment it was more like a symphony. The din was made up of an amazing number of individual sounds: a car, a truck, an air conditioner, a father's voice, a horn, an airplane, a door closing, all such sweet music to my ears.

A robin flew by.

I was able to hear the sound of both of its wings passing through the air. Each feather had its own unique sound that combined with all the other wing's feathers to make that flapping sound we all hear; and it wasn't one sound but a combination of individual sounds creating the "one" sound of wings flapping. Crazy, and yet I was able to hear all that. I had trouble with where I was hearing, it seemed as if I was hearing in two places—in my ear and also at the source of the sound. Weird and yet beautiful at the same time.

The same held true with my sense of smell.

I could smell the stench of Toronto sure enough, and as with sounds the smell too seemed made up of individual scents. The smell of a greasy spoon restaurant, the exhaust from cars, garbage, dog shit, a woman's perfume, all of it blended into the smell of Toronto. I had never been able to discern so accurately the unique essences that made up the aroma so many of us complain about and call pollution. I was actually able to smell the scent at its origin; the smell of ozone at the place where the streetcar's arm met the power line. I was confused because I also smelled the ozone in my nose.

As my bare feet touched the sidewalk I felt the energetic presence of others who had walked along the same street.

It was as if they had left a living footprint on the sidewalk—some sort of energetic history!

The twenty third Psalm played musically in my mind as the magic of life unfolded before me. It was an amazing experience, one that has always stayed with me, one that instantly began reshaping my life. I knew in that moment that all things were connected.

As I came back to my senses, I realized where I was and what I must have looked like. My ice cream cone had melted, had run down my arm and was in a pool of white mush at my feet. My hair was sticking straight out, my eyes were wide open and crazed, tears of joy pouring down my face. I am certain that if a medical doctor had happened by I would have soon found myself in a mental institute!

I dashed home, grabbed the car keys of all things and went driving! The whole experience began again and for moments I was sure I knew everything.

When I finally returned home, I realized I had locked Brigit out of the apartment. She was waiting worriedly on the front stairs of 130 Shuter Street.

In the Moment

I had no idea what had happened to me. I had no frame of reference for this experience. Every time I thought about it tears would start running down my face. Something had happened, that was certain, but what? All the knowledge I had picked up over the years, studies at university, and personal reading had not prepared me for this. I was out of my league. I was experiencing what some call a spiritual emergency.

What I Did with It Then

It was simple: I gave all the credit to Justin Sterling and his men's weekend. I did what I had been so well trained to do and gave all my personal power to the leader. I became a Sterling Men's Division junkie!

How I Think And Feel About It Now

I know by my research and personal journey towards the Great One, the Divine, God or the Truth, that this experience I had was a direct experience: an enlightenment experience, satori, samadhi or kensho. I was blessed with an opportunity to be in union with a piece of the Real. I experienced what is beyond everyday life. I got a taste of what I call God, That in Which all life exists—That Which is always here.

I learned over time that my experience was of the same kind that the great sages write about—what the great poets struggle with in putting into words. I had experienced a degree of Buddha Enlightenment.

Relating this to the Personal Growth Wheel I was working on the internal spiritual dynamic and the external belief system. I was refreshing and rebuilding my sense of spiritual personhood while at the same time I was breaking down some out-dated personal beliefs that would not hold up under the presence of my new realizations. The foundation I had built my life on was beginning to crumble. The Truth I had experienced was crushing the falseness of my mental model of my life and the world I had so innocently believed in.

It was my first step on to a path of personal spiritual growth.

What I Would Do Differently

I would find a spiritual teacher. I was entering a new and different phase of my life and I needed the loving support of a teacher who could guide me through my early stage of personal spiritual evolution. When I learned to play hockey I had a damn coach, so why would this be any different.

Notes to the Regular Guy's Handbook

12) Never give your power away to a leader.
13) Enlightenment experiences happen by Grace and are not the exclusive domain of anyone. Union with the Truth is our natural birthright; we have simply forgotten that fact.
14) Life is not as it may first seem.

6
You've Got the Wrong Man
Risking It!

The Story As I Remember It

So life went on just as it had before, but for me everything was different. There was uneasiness in my heart—things didn't feel quite right. Although living was good and my life was full, it felt like I had someone else's shoes on. I still had no idea what had happened in those moments of what seemed like other worldly experiences. I decided to get on with life as best as I could —I did and it was better than it had ever been. The sense of uneasiness would not go away though, and quietly nagged at me. I felt lost in my own life, almost as if I was living another person's life.

I made two big changes in my life as a direct result of my spiritual experiences: volunteering at a men's hospital and getting actively involved with the Sterling Men's group in Toronto.

Volunteering was my way of giving back to others. Along with my nagging sense of unrest, I had an overpowering urge to give to others in a meaningful way. I tracked down a volunteer position at the Riverdale Hospital in Toronto and each Saturday went to visit Ted, a fellow with MS. It was a profoundly rewarding experience.

I was voted team leader for the men's team I was put in during my Sterling Men's weekend. We met weekly and had all manner of contributions to make to the overall organization, enrollment being one of them.

Our team was good, yet given my feeling that Justin Sterling had transformed my life, I thought I needed to do more. So I did. I became enrollment manager, weekend assistant, volunteer supreme at every Sterling event I could. I was a Sterling groupie!

It was satisfying for the most part and I was enjoying being active in a community of men. We did community development work, put on weekend events for men and boys, created celebrations and for the most part had a good time.

I was being groomed to take over as Toronto's Men's Division Coordinator.

As Coordinator in waiting, my convocation date in New York was a ways off. I got plugged into the inner workings of the men's division, and was well connected to other division coordinators throughout eastern North America. It felt great to be so involved with the organization I credited with my new lease on life.

I had been with the Sterling movement for a year when I first noticed the peer pressure building. It began building in earnest when I found out that my wedding day in May of 1989 was on the same weekend I was to be in New York for my formal appointment as division coordinator. My wedding had been in the planning stages well before the Sterling event had been organized. I was told that I was to change my wedding plans and be in New York for my appointment.

Odd, I thought, from an organization called the Sterling Institute of Relationship. I was setting out to make formal and legal my marriage to Brigit, a most important event for my relationship. I talked with the head administrator, Joe, to get the gang to change their dates. Well, all hell broke loose and the manipulation began.

I was told that I was letting the men of Toronto down.

I was told to take charge of my woman and change the wedding plans.

I was told that Justin wouldn't be happy.

I was told to be the man I had always wanted to be.

It went on endlessly, and from all the guys in the inner circle. I was amazed at the power of the group thinking, and equally amazed at how rigid they were. No matter how I discussed it there was only one way…the Sterling way. The Sterling Cult.

I pondered my dilemma and I realized that I was being the man I'd always wanted to be and that my planned wedding was really important to me. I also realized that any good organization would support me and not handle me the way the Sterling gang did. I resolved in myself to call Joe and give him the news.

I told Joe that if this was the way they wanted to behave that I was not the man to lead the men's division. I told him clearly I was getting married on the planned date and the organization would have to live with it. Joe was angry.

Soon after I hung up I was cut off from my connection with other division leaders, from key men in the Toronto division and from the inner circle. I was a black sheep no longer to be trusted. I had apparently let the Sterling men down.

I called a meeting of the men in Toronto and told them all exactly what had happened. I let them know that if this was the price I had to pay to be division coordinator the price was too high and I was not the man to lead them. I was clear on my personal values and my personal choice. I blamed no one for the situation. I took my leave.

I got married as planned in May of 1989.

In the Moment

I was upset and proud at the same time. My involvement with the Sterling gang had been fulfilling and I had made many new friends and learned some leadership skills to boot. I was pissed off that it ended the way it did. And yet inside of me was a growing sense of personal pride; I had taken a stand that was important for me and in spite of all the pressure tactics used against me I had stood my ground. I walked away from the men's division with my head held high and felt good about myself for honouring my deepest values.

What I Did with It Then

I stayed with my men's team as we had formed a really meaningful bond and were supporting each other in making progress in our lives. I dropped out of leadership though and did not get involved in any Sterling events other than my regular team meetings.

How I Think And Feel About It Now

It was a cult no question about it. I realize in hind sight that the motto "Be the man you always wanted to be" was misstated in all Sterling's literature. There was a model of a sterling man we all had to fit into. The true operating motto was "Be the man _we_ always wanted you to be."

There were good lessons there for me—events I will always remember. The error I made was mistaking the messenger for the message.

Using some of my tools, in this case negative indicators, I began to realize something was out. The peer pressure, the manipulations, and the bullying were all signs that I was in the wrong spot and that I needed to take a close look at my values as compared to the values surrounding me. I was getting very few positive indicators.

Using the Spiritual Personal Growth Wheel I put into practice more risk taking. I took a personal stand alone which put my relationship with Sterling on the line. Looking back at it now I see that taking that stand built huge self-worth in me, I was actually courageous enough to stand up for my values. My entire way of relating to the outside world was dramatically enhanced! My sense of self-worth went up several notches and I felt stronger mentally and emotionally.

What I Would Do Differently

Pay attention to and trust my intuition!

Notes To Regular Guy's Handbook

15) Never follow a leader blindly and be wary of group-think, group-speak, and group pressure.
16) Taking a personal stand based on your deepest personal values is always worthwhile doing.
17) Be prepared to stand alone.

7
A Fork in the Road
A Spiritual Path Emerges

The Story As I Remember It

Despite the rather nasty end to my time with the Sterling group I had met some fine fellows, one of whom was Keith. I had enrolled him into the men's weekend and during our conversations he had mentioned Judy, a woman who offered mind clearing sessions and ran a weekend workshop called the Enlightenment Intensive. Keith had left her flyer with me and for some reason it captured my attention.

You see, though I had had these amazing awakenings I still carried around with me lots of emotional baggage. I was feeling the need to get some counseling or therapy or help of some sort. I struggled with this thought; I had it rigged up that, as a man, asking for help was a sign of weakness and failure.

For weeks I read over her flyer. I would pick up the telephone and then hang up the moment I had dialed the number. This pattern went on for quite a while. Finally, I could no longer stand my procrastination. I called, stayed on the line, and spoke with Judy. We arranged my first session.

So we did some therapy together and things worked well for me. I was finding my way through some of my 'stuff'. The important thing in meeting Judy though was the connections I made with her larger community. I was invited to a weekly evening group session called dyad night; a dyad is a two person supportive process that brings clarity to personal life issues.

It was there I met Anjali, who would later become my guru.

Judy and Anjali often sponsored a fellow named Skanda to facilitate workshops in Toronto. As it turned out Skanda and Satya, his wife, would be in town during the month of November (1989) putting on a series of weekend and evening events.

I signed up for as many as I qualified for.

It was amazing!

Skanda was brilliant, clear, articulate and very knowledgeable. Satya was beautiful, clever, experienced and wise. The work was wonderful. I found it stimulating and creative. It felt real and seemed to be based on spiritual truths. I learned clearing techniques, emotional trauma release, relationship evolution dyads, and extensive communication skills.

The remarkable thing was I felt at home with this new body of work, even though I had never come in contact with its teachings before. I wanted more, lots more. My hunger for Truth had been magically rekindled! I asked Anjali if she would teach me, and by letter I asked Skanda for a spiritual name.

I began studying with Anjali.

She taught me what she knew about mind clearing, about emotional trauma release, and couples relating. She taught me about communication techniques and introduced me to Enlightenment Intensives. Judy helped also by providing lots of the manuals and written material for me to duplicate so I could have my own library of the work. I poured through the material daily and read all I could that was in print. I got to know the work pretty well and began to understand the key concepts. I read all the material of the writer, Charles Berner, I could find. I copied all his tapes and listened to them whenever I could.

I was totally taken by the depth and simplicity of this body of work and the quality of people drawn to it! I had never felt so at home with anything in my life. It resonated deep within my heart and body.

I signed up for my first Intensive in the winter of 1989.

Stephan Islas was the master facilitator; it was held at a home in Stoufville, Ontario. I had no idea what I was in for, yet I was totally willing to trust Anjali's advice so I simply went and did it. It was a three-day residential retreat, vegetarian food, no coffee, no cigarettes or drugs, a strict time-schedule, and twelve or thirteen forty minute enlightenment exercises each day. We went from 6:00 am each morning to midnight each night.

All we did for the entire weekend was contemplate! Contemplation is the same as meditation. It is a process of centering the mind on a particular focus question. When we were in the exercise format with a partner we would contemplate and communicate for 5 minutes and then switch and listen to our partner for 5 minutes and go back and forth this way for 40 minutes each enlightenment exercise period. When we were not in 'dyad' we would be having eating contemplation, walking contemplation, resting contemplation or working contemplation. They even called bedtime sleeping contemplation!

"Tell me who you are", was my question, and for three days the only thing my partners would say to me was, "Tell me who you are." They would then sit there, present, and listening, saying only "thank you" when the 5-minute gong rang.

Though it was tremendously grueling and exhausting, hour after hour seeking the answer to what seemed to be such a simple question, it was also incredible!

Now the purpose, I was told, was to directly experience the object of my inquiry, in my case, me. And though it seemed like a straightforward question I really had no idea who I was and as I set out to answer this question it became painfully obvious!

Despite my not knowing, my confusion and uncertainty, my headaches and frustration, I simply stayed with the technique dyad after dyad. Even though I had no idea where this was all going, nor what the result might be, I plodded along gong after gong. Emotions, thoughts, body aches, hallucinations, boredom all came to visit me during my work towards the elusive goal called enlightenment.

We were well into the second morning and out on an hour long walking contemplation when something unusual happened. I don't remember much of what happened nor how it occurred, but in a flash I had been physically knocked backward into the snow several feet from where I had been standing. Tears were pouring down my face. I had a splitting headache. In that instant I knew I was the space between all things and the tick between the seconds. It was as if I was everything and nothing all at the same time. It was as if I had always existed and always would.

I had no idea what had just happened, so I struggled to my feet and kept on going with the technique. But it kept coming up, "the space between all things, the tick between the seconds." I shared my experience with one of the staff members and he simply asked, "Who's noticing the space or the tick?" I think he missed it and simply sent me off chasing my tail, so to speak. Not knowing much about enlightenment, I just kept doing the technique. I listened intently to the master facilitator's lectures and his regular encouragement.

The intensive went on and so did I. The emotions, the boredom, the weird thoughts, the hallucinations, the extended periods of no man's land, and my sore butt were unrelenting.

On the final day during evening walking contemplation I was struck with another direct experience. This time it was more like a gentle spring breeze than the hammer-like hit that struck me a day earlier. It was a quiet little opening; I got I was simply of God. My mind made up that I was a child of God—"I am a child of God," is how I reported it to my next dyad partner.

Both experiences, though different, had one thing in common. For a moment there was nothing except me and the Truth. Much like I had vanished and everything in my world had vanished too. For an instant there just was something that included everything but was nothing in the same moment. It was weird, and yet seemed more real than life itself.

My first intensive was over.

There was a brief sharing and closing ceremony, we had a delicious snack and then we all packed up, hopped into our cars and drove home. As bizarre as it may seem this enlightenment intensive felt like home to me. Though confused and puzzled by what had happened, I knew this was the first step towards a new and different life.

In the Moment

I really had no idea what to do with my first enlightenment intensive experience. I had some weird things happen during this first step into the ring of spiritual fire. I had a strong urge to do more and yet I wasn't quite sure why. Something had in fact shifted inside me, but I couldn't figure out what it was. I yearned for more of what I had experienced on my first Intensive.

I remember playing hockey as a young boy growing up in Montreal. I could never get enough. I played hockey every chance I could. I watched it on television, I dreamed about it, I played it every season of the year. That feeling of YES for hockey was the same feeling I was experiencing for the Enlightenment Intensive—for the Truth.

What I Did with It Then

I simply wrote about it all in my journal; marked it down to experience and left it alone. I signed up to staff my first intensive with Judy and continued my studies with Anjali.

Months later I was driving up to the intensive site with Judy. I told her the stories of my first intensive. She pulled the car over to the side of the road and listened intently to my tales. I also told her about my evening after the men's weekend; the experiences I wrote about after having sex with Brigit that Monday evening.

As I told the tales of those experiences she paid even more attention. It turned out, according to her, I appeared to have had several direct experiences; moments of union with Truth.

With her expert help I continued to flush out the fullness of my experiences, and all of a sudden I was reliving them again! It was such a relief to be sharing these moments with someone who could understand what had happened, someone who could give me some feedback and appropriate guidance and support.

As it turned out I wasn't going crazy after all!

How I Think and Feel About It Now

Looking back at my first intensive I realize how right it was for me. The process, the technique, the desire for 'knowing' the Truth, all resonated deeply with me. I know that this was my first major step towards my own personal spiritual growth, towards my own awakening.

Using the Personal Spiritual Growth Wheel as a guide again, it is easy to see I was working on my inner sense of spirituality while outwardly I was focusing on two of the quadrants, communication and beliefs. The intensive taught only a four step meditation process, no dogma at all, so I had a very good look at my personal belief system. Through the process I was able to let go of many of my beliefs that were not based in Truth. Many ideas I had about myself and others were blown apart and found wanting.

As I continued to work with the technique I was feeding my spirit and building inner personal strength, and deepening faith in myself. The entire intensive process was a very positive experience and over time it was easy to notice the many positive changes in my life.

In looking back it was clear I had found a path of study that really worked for me and I made the conscious decision to continue with my studies and practices of this body of growth work.

What I Would Do Differently

I would have checked out with the intensive staff much more thoroughly what had happened for me. I was still in a place of not fully taking care of myself and my experiences. I would be more clear and direct and ask for the support and direction I knew I needed. I would connect with the master facilitator more regularly to get guidance and support.

Notes to the Regular Guy's Handbook

18) Any idea you have about what enlightenment looks like or how it happens is wrong.
19) Intention is a powerful force. The feeling of determination, that sense of really meaning it can move mountains.

8
It's Time to Go
Letting Go of a Career

The Story As I Remember It

Since June 20th, 1988 many things had changed in my life, I should say in my private life, because not much had really changed in my work world. I had found a spiritual path and joined in a community of people living life spiritually; I had stopped drinking and doing drugs. All else, though, was pretty much the same.

I still worked for Burns Fry Limited; I still played squash and golf; I still did most things I had learned to identify myself by. I dressed the same, spoke the same old way, and drove my Ford MerKur as fast as I usually did. I basically lived as I always had. Though my understanding about myself, life, and others was changing, my public life was not.

On a very subtle level somewhere inside me was a growing seed of discontent with how I was living my life. It had actually started the day I finished my men's weekend, but the feeling was so minute it went unnoticed by me. The feeling of dissatisfaction continued its growth, though, and each minor change I made in my inner life added to the feeling of tension.

The big push came when I received my spiritual name from Skanda.

It was January of 1990.

I had asked for my name several months earlier and had almost resigned myself to the fact that Skanda was either too busy or had forgotten entirely about my request for a 'name'. Well, as it turned out, he had remembered and the envelope from Australia that I had just taken out of my mailbox attested to that fact.

I carried the mail upstairs to my second floor apartment shaking with both nervousness and anticipation. I knew my spiritual name would be inside and for some strange reason couldn't bear the thought of finally knowing it. So I headed for the bathroom, letter in hand, and sat nervously in the privacy of a locked privy!

I am not sure how long I sat there talking myself into opening the letter, hands shaking and heart beating. It must have been at least a half-hour. At any rate I remember saying to myself, "Come on, open the darn letter!" So open it I did.

The first couple of paragraphs were acknowledging my request, explaining the significance of taking on a spiritual name and a bit about the lineage I was entering.

Skanda then went into his choice of name for me. He wrote:

> *In Sanskrit, the name for divine love or worship is bhakti. Bhaktis love God with their heart, and this love and their expression of it leads them to the Divine itself. Others empha-size study of truth, or practicing techniques (the jnani and the karmi), but the bhakti follows the heart mainly. The fulfill-ment of this process is a stage beyond bhakti, which is the same as union with Truth or samadhi, or the complete fulfillment of life. One who has cultivated the path of the heart and suc-ceeded to final union, is called a parabhakti, and this is the name I give you.*
>
> *Parabhakti.*

I wept, and wept deeply, for this was the first time in my life I had felt truly seen and truly named. The name Parabhakti resonated so deeply in my heart I was immediately filled with joy.

Over the next days and weeks I continued to read the letter and remind myself of my new name. I began to ask close friends, my wife, Anjali, and the enlightenment community to call me by my Sanskrit name, Parabhakti. I was unwilling or unable to do the same at the office and there I carried on as Stephen Lloyd Garrett.

The letter still hangs over my altar to this day as a reminder of my deepest calling.

That feeling of something not being quite right in my life now became much more pronounced. You see I had been spotted, named, and called to live a deeper life. As I looked at how I earned money, what I did for a living, it became more intolerable each day. I was a money market trader. I earned a living by buying and selling short-term investments for profit. By day I lived as a right wing capitalist. In my private life I was a closet spiritualist. The juxtaposition I found myself in was becoming increasingly difficult to maintain.

Something had to give.

For the next several months I continued to live my dual life. By day I put in time with Burns Fry and toiled away at the corner of King and Bay Streets on the 50th floor of First Canadian Place, watching computer screens, talking to clients and setting up short-term money market deals.

By night I poured over all the spiritual material I could find, books, manuals, scripture and autobiographies of as many great saints as I could find. My bedside table looked like a who's who of the spiritual growth movement. Krishnamurti, Ram Dass, Andrew Cohen, Da Free John, Ken Wilber, Gandhi, Francesco, and Jesus. The Tao, Koran, Bible and studies of the seven major world religions and all of Yogeshwar Muni's work lay stacked neatly on the floor by my bed. Stuart Wilde, Carlos Castenadas, and Dan Millman, joined the growing pile of 'teachers'.

By mid March it all became insufferable. The tension between my growing spiritual beliefs and my daily life was becoming too intense to bear. It was time for something to give. I needed to make a change in my life, for the new awareness I had been developing was out of harmony with how I was living. The big city life, big career job all the glitter of the American dream was no longer it for me.

I had to quit.

I made the internal decision months before I could even begin to think of making it public.

I had lived in Vancouver on and off over the years and had always been drawn to live there full time. I visited the Sunshine Coast often and felt a real pull to live in a coastal rural community. So, I opened a bank account with the Royal Bank there and began sending money to my new home! I started to design the house I wanted to build for Brigit and me. I fantasized about building a new career working with people somehow. I had all this exciting stuff going on in the inside but still lived my old ways. I felt almost schizophrenic.

One day I felt so close to exploding I knew the time had come. I knew I had to talk to Mark, my boss. I was so afraid to do it, to make that major commitment to change my life. Each morning I promised myself I would talk with him. And each afternoon walking home I was disappointed that I hadn't.

Finally one day just before lunch hour I just got up, full of fear and apprehension I walked up to Mark's office door and asked for 5 minutes of his time. Before I knew it the words were out of my mouth, "Mark I am living a lie, I am no longer the right guy for this job. Things have changed in my life and I need to quit. Someone more dedicated to the business needs to be in my chair." Mark asked for the lunch hour to consider my resignation.

After lunch I was called into his office and it was made official: I would finish my career of 23 years in two weeks. In fourteen days I would be a free, unemployed man and my dreams of moving to a small rural community on the West Coast of Canada could be acted on.

That afternoon I walked home with a hop in my step and a huge smile on my face. Now I could begin to act on the daydreaming I had been doing for the past months. Now Brigit and I could begin to plan our new life and our adventure of leaving Toronto for the romantic call of rural, coastal British Columbia.

For me a new life had just begun.

In the Moment

I was so excited about my new spiritual life and beliefs it was as if I was living in some sort of dream state. It felt great and weird at the same time. I had no idea how significant a change I was making, nor what the lessons along the way would look like. All I really knew was how relieved I was to be out of the closet so I could try to live from my new and deeper spiritual understanding of life. I had no sense of how unusual my decision was, but I just knew I had to make big changes in the way I lived, earned money, and related to others.

What I Did with It Then

I just followed my logical mind like I had done throughout my banking and investment career, I planned my way ahead. We picked a departure date, worked on the building plans for our home, researched the real estate market on the Sunshine Coast, discussed our new business plans, and created a vision for how things would evolve for us. We also sold our sports car, all of our furniture and much of our 'stuff'. We bought a big burgundy van we affectionately called Bud, packed her up, held a good-bye party, and left for the West Coast in early April, 1990.

How I Think and Feel About It Now

Had I realized then just how huge a change I was making and what would be coming my way over the next years as I moved from capitalism to spiritualism I don't think I would have left the safety of Bay Street. The changes were so dramatic and so deep, the calling to serve so loud that during the next few years I often felt out of control in my own life. I realize now what an act of faith and courage it was for me to take control of my own life and direct it where I wanted to go. It was no small step.

That being said, my life was full of positive indicators. I was happy in my life, I had a lot more personal energy, and I was looking forward to my new plans. I was healthier and living a much cleaner life.

Again I practiced taking risks, and as a result my relationship with others in my life was improving. I was a better communicator, my negative self talk or mind chatter was lessening, and I felt a whole lot better about myself.

Inwardly my mind and all the usual chatter was more calm. My sense of spirituality was much improved. I was more expressive with my emotions in a healthy way, and I was very physically fit.

All in all, things were going well in the life of Parabhakti. I had begun to master my own life!

What I Would Do Differently

I wouldn't wait so long to act on the inner decision I had made. I would move from planning to action much more quickly. I wouldn't waste time second guessing myself.

Notes to the Regular Guy's Handbook

20) Personal change and growth is risky business. Be willing for your entire life to change.

21) Listen to your inner voice, trust your intuition, and you will most often know what to do.

22) Be patient with yourself, because significant change takes time. Make it a project not a chore.

9

The Spirit Moves Them West
From Riches to Rags

The Story As I Remember It

My last year's income was $155,000.00 (1989). Remember that figure.

The trip out west was grand! It felt so good to have all my stuff in one GMC van. No bosses, no deadlines to meet, and freedom to do what I wanted and go wherever the mood took me. I hadn't felt this free and this alive since I was a young boy on summer vacation back in the 60s.

We meandered through Ontario and found our way to Sioux Lookout to visit an old friend. We ambled through the prairies to Edmonton where we stayed with family and renewed our old friendships. Brigit was raised there and I had spent 5 years in Edmonton in the early 80s working for the Treasury Department of the Alberta Government. We lazily made our way through the Canadian Rockies and poured ourselves out into the Lower Mainland through Hope and down to Vancouver and the coast.

Once on the Sunshine Coast, just a short way west of Vancouver, we putted along the coast highway. We drove along checking out all the campsites looking for a place to hang our hats while we searched for a place to live. It was busy on the coast and most hotels and campsites were sold out. We drove from Gibsons through Roberts Creek, past Sechelt and beyond Halfmoon Bay—no vacancies.

Finally, as we neared the top of the peninsula we happened on Garden Bay and Wally Nowak's Fisherman's Resort; he had a campsite available. We took it and set up shop.

Some time the next morning Wally, who had just purchased the resort, asked, "You looking for work?"

"Sure, what do you have in mind?" I responded, a bit surprised at his forthright request.

"I need a dock-boy for the summer and fall. I'll pay you cash at $8.00 an hour," Wally offered.

"All right then, you've got yourself a dock-boy!" I had changed from a department manager of one of Canada's premier investment firms on 'Bay Street' to dock-boy at a tourist resort in Garden Bay in a matter of months.

And so my new life began.

Within days we had found a cozy basement apartment to live in. Brigit had found a retail spot to set up her massage business and life in rural BC was taking shape for us. We began making friends and developing a bit of a social life.

We started searching for our land.

Brigit and I had created a visual collage of what our new home and property would look like, so we had a strong image of what the piece of property would need to offer; southern exposure, space for large gardens, close to the water, and private. I also had a dream prior to leaving Toronto that we would know the right piece of land by something yellow! As a corporate fellow I had trouble admitting it, but I did have a premonition, an intuitive sense of something yet to come. Something yellow would indicate the right piece of land to buy. I was hoping for something more specific than that as a clue, but yellow was all I got as a hint.

For months we searched the coast for the perfect piece of land, and as each unsuccessful visit came and went our hopes for the ideal property began to fade. Finally one day I said, "Fuck it! I've had enough of trekking through the forests, swamps and hills of this damn place. If you want land, you find it!"

The next day Brigit came home excited as all be. "I found it!" she exclaimed with more pep and gusto than I had seen in her for months. "It's been right under our noses all along." She grabbed me and we drove back towards the highway on Garden Bay road to a little side street just off the lake called Elliot Road. 5146 Elliot Road was for sale!

As we explored the 1 1/2 acre site we began to fall in love with it. Right size. Southern exposure. Nice site for the house with a view of Garden Bay Lake and Mount Daniel. Excellent site for a garden. Lots of privacy. After all the searching we had done over the past 5 months, had we finally found the site of our future home?

"How did you know this place was for sale?" I asked.

"Oh, there is a sign down there hanging from a tree branch above the road," Brigit was quick to respond.

"Where?"

"Just there." She pointed.

I headed in the direction she had motioned towards and soon found the hand painted sign. "For Sale. Call…" I could barely believe my eyes.

"Brigit, look at this!" I urged.

The sign was hand painted in bright yellow paint!

We bought the property, finished the design and plans for the house, found Ted Woodard a master carpenter who led the building of the home. By December 1990 the house was well under way.

At the end of the year I took stock of what had changed in my life over the past twelve months:

- ✓ quit a career of some twenty-three years
- ✓ married Brigit
- ✓ sold almost all my worldly possession
- ✓ moved from the bustle of Toronto to the quietness of Garden Bay, BC
- ✓ left my family, extended family and circle of friends behind in urban Canada and
- ✓ had exchanged and income of $155,000 for a wage of $12,000 for my first year in the country

In the Moment

I didn't really notice what I had accomplished in the past year, nor did I take time to celebrate my accomplishments. I just noticed how much was left to do on the house, what I needed to do to find more work in social services, and what was left to accomplish in my life. I did what I always had done, kept my sights on my goals and continued plodding towards them.

What I Did with It Then

I just kept going, banging nails, looking for better opportunities in social services, and finding ways to be more involved in my community.

How I Think and Feel About It Now

It took great courage to change my life as radically as I did.

I needed to spend more time working on my inner self and all the transitions I was going through personally. I needed to find ways to celebrate my successes. I needed to invest some time in doing my inner work; I was too busy with tasks and chores and was overly goal focused. I realize now that I was beginning to slip back into old habits. Though I was no longer on Bay Street doing what I had done for years, my beliefs remained the same. I just acted them out differently. I wasn't paying close enough attention to my innermost feelings and taking good care of my spirit. Old habits die hard.

What I Would Do Differently

Celebrate my accomplishments!

I would take the time to enjoy my successes. I would buy myself a small gift or celebrate with friends. I would make sure I found ways to acknowledge what I had achieved. In short I would give myself credit for those things I had accomplished.

Notes to the Regular Guy's Handbook

23) Romantic ideas are wonderful, but be prepared for the practical issues that make them a reality.
24) Changing your life is not for the faint of heart; it takes guts!
25) Celebrate your successes!

10

Addicted to What?
The Struggle to Stay with My Dream

The Story As I Remember It

So the adventure continued. It was well into January 1991, the snow had just melted and spring, at least on the Sunshine Coast, was well on its way.

Ted and I were working on the house and had it close to lockup by late February. I had found a couple of part time jobs in the social services field that approximated full time work. Brigit's private massage practice was doing well and we had made a nice circle of new friends. All seemed well, at least from the outside.

Little things were beginning to piss me off though. The tight quarters of the trailer we were living in as we built the home. Frozen water pipes and a cold outhouse. Not having much money and having nowhere to spend it was another. Pay cheque to pay cheque living in rural BC was not all it was made out to be; I began thinking about 'Bay Street' and my old life.

Silk ties, my sports car, a squash game, and a warm toilet to sit on all came to mind. A night out at the theatre. A nice bottle of red wine at a funky restaurant. Some damn street lights, of all things. The excitement of the markets, the noise of the big city and a regular supply of bigger pay cheques, those pay cheques I used to take for granted. I missed it all.

I wanted to go back. I really wanted to go back. I had enough of rural living, building a house, developing new friends, and most of all doing without all the things I had become so accustomed to.

I remember feeling very anxious, emotional, and almost physically ill as I struggled to stay with my dream of a new life in the country. I spoke with

Brigit about it, thank God, and she totally supported my staying with it, which helped to a degree, but the thoughts kept pouring through my mind. 'Bay Street' was calling loudly to me.

It came to me one night in April that I need to do something to let go of the past life I used to live. It was as if I still had one foot in Toronto, even thought the bulk of me was in Garden Bay. I realized that I had never really let go of my old life in the banking and investment business. I had simply left Toronto and my old job for Garden Bay and a new job.

As I put my attention on what changes I had gone through, I realized I needed to do some sort of ceremony to be finished with the old and welcome in the new. I needed to find a couple of men to help me create this ceremony, to find a suitable outdoor location and help with the planning of the ritual.

A bonfire by a creek somewhere in the woods.

Private.

Two men as support.

A ceremony that would see me say good-bye to the person I used to be in Toronto and to welcome the person I was now on the Sunshine Coast.

Clark and Leylan, two men I had come to know, both good men, agreed to help me out. Leylan knew the woods well and was into ritual and ceremony; Clark was a member of my men's team on the coast and was into personal growth.

Leylan found the site. Clark helped me create the ritual.

We agreed on a meeting place, a date and time, and a location. Leylan would take care of the firewood and the use of the creek. Clark would build the fire and keep it safe and contained. I would gather personal items that would represent my past life. Both men would witness the ritual and do what they felt appropriate to support me.

The morning of the ceremony arrived and I was within a whisker of calling both guys and canceling out. I was scared shitless. I reminded myself of my men's weekend way back in 1988, sucked up my courage and carried on as planned.

We meet at a spot just off the highway, parked our cars, and followed Leylan into the woods towards the site he had found for the ritual. We walked quietly onwards, silently carrying our packs full of the needed materials. We had agreed that there would be little talking. Only necessary words to do with the ritual and its organization would be spoken.

We arrived at an isolated and private clearing. It was only a few feet from a creek running swollen with spring runoff from the mountains above. The water would be breathtakingly cold. Clark built the fire, Leylan gathered cedar boughs, and I prepared myself for the ceremony. I dressed in a suit and tie that I used to wear for work in Toronto. I had a black bodysuit on underneath.

Leylan was prepared, the fire was roaring and we began.

As I took off each article of my Bay Street 'uniform' I placed it into the fire speaking out loud what it represented for me. The tie was the stranglehold the greed of money had on me. The suit jacket was the mask I had to wear to cover my true self and to be admitted to the Bay Street game. So it went, belt, pants, socks, shoes and underwear. Each piece of clothing burning to nothingness.

I sat there dressed only in a black bodysuit.

I sat there as my own death.

It was silent.

I removed the bodysuit and headed towards the creek, Clark and Leylan following my example. We all stood naked in the creek. I lowered my body into the creek face first and did pushups in and out of the freezing water. Leylan whisked my back with cedar boughs and Clark joined me in cleansing his body in the icy stream. It was a noisy affair, yelps and screams streaming from my mouth—no words, just guttural sounds and energy coming from deep within my body.

Finally, I was done, having had enough of the cold and the cedar boughs. I found my way back to the fire, bundled up in a blanket, curled up by the fire and wept.

Not a word was spoken.

We all dressed in silence. Clark doused the fire, Leylan packed our bags, we walked back to the parking spot. I hugged both men. They got into their trucks and drove off. I got into mine and drove slowly northward up highway 101 to my home in Garden Bay.

In the Moment

I didn't think much of it at the time. It was just a ritual for God's sake! After all, what good would it do to burn a bunch of silly clothes and bath naked in a freezing cold creek? However, I did notice a shift in my attitude, an increase in my energy to find a better social services job and complete building my dream home.

What I Did with It Then

I didn't talk much about the ceremony, in fact I keep it private. Only Clark, Leylan and I knew about it. I wrote about it in my personal journal and left it at that. This is how it should have been. It was a personal ritual, a sacred ceremony and needed to be kept private, not damaged by too much talk and exposure.

How I Think and Feel About It Now

Looking back I now realize what an important event the ritual actually was. It was a powerful thing to do; it fundamentally changed me. It was a piece of sacred spiritual work that fully supported my personal development. Yes, there was effort around letting go of my thoughts, feelings and emotions, but more so it was an acknowledgement of the deep spiritual side of my life.

I fully let go of my attachment to my Bay Street way of life. My ceremony completed a twenty-three year cycle. It was the ending I needed before I truly was able to embrace my new beginning. By creating this ritual and carrying it out I put the universe on notice that I was ready for a fresh start!

What I Would Do Differently

I would plan and organize the ritual earlier, when I first started to notice the resentment building up in my body. I would act more quickly.

Notes to the Regular Guy's Handbook

26) There is an important place for ritual in a man's life.
27) Changing a lifestyle is more than simply changing your address.
28) Men need the support of other good men.

11
Then Came the Boys
Spiritual Growth, Add Two Children and Stir

The Story As I Remember It

Back in 1989 Brigit and I had created a goal collage that 'pictured' the life we wanted to create for ourselves in our new rural environment. It hung on a wall in our walk-in closet so we could see it each day.

The house was completed for the most part and we moved in on the 1st of May, 1991. I had taken on a couple of employment contracts in social services in Sechelt and continued my spiritual training with Anjali via mail. I took and staffed some Enlightenment Intensives in Vancouver. Brigit's business was flourishing. All was well and the dream we had created for ourselves was unfolding nicely.

Daily I found ways to meditate and pray. I found creative ways to study the work Anjali and Skanda had introduced me to. Tapes of many of Skanda's training workshops and those of his guru filled my car's glove box. I listened to them each day as I drove the 45 kilometers to my job in Sechelt. Whenever there was an intensive or workshop in Vancouver based on this work I was there either as staff or as participant.

I continued to work around the house, completing the painting, laying wood flooring, and building a root cellar. I put in gardens, planted fruit trees and berry bushes. I loved it; and when I compared what we had created on the property to the pictures in the goal collage it was amazing to see how close the match was.

We were living a dream life it seemed, spiritual, in nature, our own owner-built home, and both earning a living working with people.

I had just completed an Enlightenment Intensive; as I recall it was a two-week intensive back east with Anjali. She mastered the intensive and I was her senior monitor. It was an amazing experience and deeply spiritual for me. God, the Truth, the Divine, Life, was everywhere to be experienced. It was like living in a monastery!

I returned to Garden Bay in a very open and present space. I felt so alive in each moment. I was vital, aware, and very clear. I found Brigit amazingly attractive. She appeared to me more like a Goddess than ever before. I remember saying to her, "If we make love tonight we are going to make a baby boy." I am not sure where that came from, but on some deep level I knew that we were about to create life through our love making.

And we did.

Though Brigit thought it was a fluke that I had called it right, I *knew* there was no fluke involved. I was simply so present and so clear in that moment I just 'knew' a baby boy was going to be created. As the pregnancy advanced so did my relationship with my yet to be born son. I marveled at the way Brigit's body adjusted and changed, surrendering to the growth of the baby. Her hips opening, her breasts preparing to feed the child, her ribs adjusting to the ever bulging belly. I had a whole new appreciation for Brigit and for women.

The day finally arrived. The labour, and I now understand why they call it that, was 36 hours long, Brigit was heroic, her strength and courage amazed me. In the end it all seemed like a timeless moment.

Oliver was born.

He took his first breath, and claimed residency in his body. With my soft eyes I could see his spirit settling in for this life in his body. Tears of joy streamed down my face. It was magical.

When the nursing staff had finished cleaning him up, dressing him and wrapping Oliver in a warm and snuggly blanket, I asked to hold him. I took him away from the birthing room. For the first time we sat together in the hallway of St. Mary's Hospital in Sechelt, British Columbia.

"Oliver, I am so glad you are here. Welcome to this world. I am your father, my name is Parabhakti. I am here for you." The words just came out of my mouth; I wept with joy that I was able to welcome him to this new life. I knew he did not understand the words I spoke, yet I knew he could 'feel' my welcome.

My life had changed yet again, and within a couple of years we were greeted with the birth of Benjamin, our second son and another change in our life.

I was amazed again by the capacity of Brigit to so totally surrender to the life force and the growing human in her belly. The evolution was familiar, the swelling belly, the larger breasts, and the opening hips. The life energy though was different and my relationship to the unborn baby was also different. I was not certain of the gender. I related to the child much as I did the first time through, singing and talking to the baby on a regular basis.

Benjamin W. was born also after 36 hours of labour, also with his umbilical cord around his neck, and also as a baby boy. I welcomed him to his new life and shared with him my name and my role in his life. Now we were four.

My spiritual practice continued throughout this period of family change. I continued my studies, I took and staffed intensives. I sponsored Anjali to come west to teach, give personal counseling sessions, and deliver Enlightenment Intensives to people on the Sunshine Coast.

I continued my work in social services, and became involved in hospice work. I trained as a specialist in conflict resolution and took a one-year program to develop my skills as a trainer and facilitator. I had a full life and it was glorious.

In the Moment

I was having fun. My life was full, I was learning, working and growing. My family was full and alive. We had accomplished many goals we had set for ourselves and I was feeling comfortable in my new life.

What I Did with It Then

I just enjoyed my life. I didn't think too much about the future. I was busy with my family life, my work life was challenging, and my spiritual life was full and satisfying. I allowed myself to slip into a sense of confidence and comfort. To be truthful I slipped into a type of spiritual automatic pilot, I lost my edge and became complacent. In a way I stopped growing spiritually and personally.

How I Think and Feel About It Now

I realize looking back that I had become too comfortable in my life. I had not set any new goals for myself, nor had we for ourselves as a couple. I was very active with work and in my community, though I didn't notice it in the moment I was beginning to fall asleep in my life. I wasn't paying attention. The seeds of upset and change were being sown and I failed to realize it. I stopped paying attention to all the practices that had improved my life. I ignored the small negative indicators and did not reflect on my life by using the tools I had come to trust.

What I Would Do Differently

I would surround myself with good men, men who would help me stay committed to my personal goals and continually stretching myself. I would review my personal goals and life's mission and reset them yearly. I would review with my wife what we were committed to as a couple.

Notes to the Regular Guy's Handbook

29) Support your woman fully during pregnancy no matter what.
30) Be there for your newborn child, welcome them to their new life and do it with heart.
31) Having goals is important for a man's health. Living his purpose is a matter of life and death.

12

Made in the Shade?
My World Comes Crashing Down

The Story As I Remember It

Work was good. I had taken on a new employment contract with the local health council as their transitional administrative coordinator. I was challenged to my full capacity and loved it. Creating a health and management plan for our local community and region was the most significant piece of work I had ever taken on. I was also still active as a board member on several local community organizations.

I had completed two diploma programs over the years, one in adult education, another in conflict resolution. I was looking around for a master's degree program I could sink my teeth into.

I had also run for public office and was considering another campaign as I felt the call to contribute further to my community.

I was having fun with my children.

I continued with my spiritual growth by taking more intensives more personal growth workshops and furthered my training with Anjali.

My life was working. I became comfortable in it, almost complacent. It felt a bit like I had gone back to sleep though. Despite my earlier awakenings and my personal growth work I was falling back to the automatic pilot routine—it was subtle—I didn't even notice it.

I was busy and didn't notice the slight rift developing between Brigit and me. We were growing apart slowly. The incremental changes were barely noticeable. I was continuing with my spiritual growth and becoming less like the man she married. Brigit was continuing with her massage therapy business and full on as mom. I think she was wanting the old me back, the Bay Street money making party guy.

There were some signs that we were in the early throws of relationship trouble and I was either unwilling or unable to notice them. Brigit began asking if we could go to couples counseling. She began telling me that she felt drawn to other men, though she was not acting on it. It felt as though we had drifted miles apart; sex was infrequent.

I wrote these issues off to postpartum depression, though I never mentioned it to Brigit. I endured the lack of sex, the feeling of separation and the other signs as simply part of the process of Brigit adjusting to family life with two boys. I had children from my first marriage and knew the challenges of getting used to being a full time parent. I got more fully involved in my work life, and community life.

On the surface it looked like we were the perfect family, wonderful photographs and celebrations, lots of friends, a great home and organic gardens. Yet lurking underneath it all was an imminent crash.

At some point that year Brigit made an internal choice that it was over. It was not spoken out loud, but she was on her way out. The relationship continued to become more distant and more unreal. The beginning of the end was upon us even though neither one of us was speaking about it.

Some time during the early fall of 1995 the end began to make itself clear. I had been left before by a woman; my first wife had left me for another man back in 1977. I knew the feelings, that kind of intuitive sense that something was afoot. I couldn't put my finger on it but something was out. Brigit was no longer interested in me in any way. Her life energy, including her sexual energy was going elsewhere and I knew that. I was simply too afraid to confront it.

She had started giving massage sessions to a family up Ruby Lake way. They had been in a bad car accident. It all seemed innocent at the outset, house calls being a part of Brigit's massage therapy business. I didn't pay much attention to it.

As time went on, though, the sessions began taking longer and Brigit was spending a good deal of time with this family. The distant feeling in our relationship was likely a large contributor to her seeking attention and love elsewhere. The more separate I felt, the more I poured myself into my work and the more she sought attention from others.

Though it all makes some kind of sense in hindsight, in the moment all I knew was that things felt terrible and were slipping from bad to worse. She wanted us to go for counseling and I didn't. I started paying more attention to her needs and she rejected my efforts. The relationship was in critical condition and we were not at all addressing it.

As time went on our relationship turned into a pile of shit. I started to feel the loss and began to do whatever I could to keep her. She was not at all open to my overtures though and continued to seek relationship satisfaction elsewhere. Even though we never spoke it out loud we both knew on some level she was leaving and it was just a matter of time.

It became unbearable.

I turned into a spineless yes man, willing to do anything to keep the relationship alive. I agreed to counseling, though by that time it was too late and my willingness to work it out fell on deaf ears. I quit all my outside activities and became a homebody, doing anything I could to make it up to her. It was too late.

My marriage was over.

March 2, 1996 was the night I had planned Brigit's birthday party. I had originally organized it with some restaurant friends of mine in Sechelt. We had friends up and down the coast and Sechelt was the halfway point. Brigit though demanded that we hold it at Ruby Lake Resort and so it was.

All our friends were there and the celebration began. Everything seemed fine at first, yet something was not quite right. Throughout the evening people started leaving; I couldn't figure it out. People were talking about something and I knew nothing of what was happening. I felt like I was living in a cone of silence. Something was going on but I was totally in the dark.

The evening went on; Brigit seemed to be really enjoying herself, dancing, chatting and having fun. I was feeling totally confused, and shut out of what seemed to be a party within a party. Around midnight when things had wound down to a bare few, I mentioned I would like to leave and call it a night; Brigit agreed and said she would be right out.

Forty minutes later she joined me in the car. We drove home in silence.

Sunday morning came early. I was in the kitchen getting breakfast ready. We had several friends who had stayed over instead of facing a long drive down the coast late at night.

Michele came into the kitchen. I said good morning and prepared for a warm hug as we had been good friends for 5 or 6 years. Instead Michele burst into tears and ran out of the kitchen, down the front stairs and off down the street. Her husband Terry looked glum and didn't offer any explanation. I was stunned, confused, and frightened.

I took off down the street and found Michele sitting on the dock at the foot of Elliot Road. She was looking out over Garden Bay Lake, weeping deeply. She would not say a word to me about what was going on aside from saying I needed to talk with Brigit.

Returning to the house I found Brigit and my friend Vivian talking privately in our bedroom. As I entered the room the conversation ended abruptly. I confronted Brigit and demanded to know what the hell was going on. She simply told me in a rather smug way that she was not prepared to discuss it. Even when I pressed her for the truth citing what was happening with Michele and what I sensed was going on with Vivian she held strong to her commitment not to talk with me about it.

It was horrible.

It went on all day until I finally stormed out of the house with Oliver and went walking to Katherine Lake. An hour or two later Brigit showed up with Ben in tow. She laid the truth on me.

She was leaving.

I played well the role of a wimp, lots of heart and no spine.

I simply let her go. My wife was leaving me for another man and all I could muster was, "I will wait for you to check him out, take your time, just don't fuck him, and I will be glad to take you back."

The ending was ugly, nasty and clandestine. It dragged on for many months before the honest truth came out. The secrecy, not knowing who this other man was drove me crazy until finally one day I broke down and really fell apart emotionally. I was in a total rage. At that point a good friend of mine could no longer stand to see me in so much pain. He chose then to break the silence and tell me exactly what had gone on.

I learned that Brigit had fallen for a man who lived at and owned Ruby Lake Resort and that she had told many of our friends about it the evening of her birthday party.

As I let the new information in it all began to make sense. Oddly enough I felt relieved.

In the Moment

I was devastated. My heart was broken, my dreams were smashed. I lost the joy of having my boys seven days a week. I lost my home and gardens. I lost it all. My emotional state was fragile, my self esteem shattered and my old nasty negative self-talk was ruling the day. I was in total reactivity and spiraling down into a dark nasty shit hole. All I did was bitch and complain about how awful it was, and how rotten Brigit was being.

What I Did with It Then

I just reacted. I was living my life in a total daze. It was all I could do to get through each day one at a time. I began to isolate myself and go it alone. All the things I had accomplished over the past years of spiritual practice seemed to disappear. I became small in my life again, reactive and very much out of touch with my own personal power. All my old beliefs and patterns seemed to re-emerge. I was at the mercy of my mind!

Left by a woman, again. Fuck!

I am not good enough. I am not lovable. Don't trust men. The holy trinity of my mind, the three core beliefs I had built my life upon, were in a state of heightened alert. My ego was back in power and ruling the day yet again.

How I Think and Feel About It Now

I realize in hindsight that this crisis was another learning opportunity for me. Though I spent the first three or four months in shock and disbelief, I did ultimately use the break-up as fodder for my own personal growth. I took personal responsibility for my lot in life and began to look at how I had created this disaster. What had I done to push Brigit away? How had I behaved that would result in Brigit leaving me for another man?

I did therapy sessions, group processes, weekend workshops, retreats and meditations to search deeply for the answers. I struggled with my self esteem, my belief systems, and how I communicated with others. I looked at it all!

I found some answers.

What I Would Do Differently

I would have done only one thing differently. I would have taken a much more protective stand. I would not have let my wife leave so easily. I would have been more forceful and direct. I would have taken a strong approach and told her, 'No, this won't do!' I would have tracked down the other man and delivered an aggressive message to him too! "You stay the fuck away from my wife or I'll kill you!"

I would pay much more attention to my wife's complaints and find ways to address them more quickly.

Notes to the Regular Guy's Handbook

32) A man needs to take a strong stand when it comes to his family.
33) Pay attention to what is really going on in your life, notice the signals your partner is giving you—and trust your intuition.

13
Fuck You God!
Life After Death

The Story As I Remember It

Well I am not sure when it happened but it did.

I turned away from my spiritual practice and fell right back into the safety of work. On some level I figured that if this separation from wife and family was the reward I got for spiritual practice and serving others, then fuck it. The pain and loss was way too much, and if this was what God had in mind for me I wasn't sticking around.

Spiritually, I checked out.

Shortly after my marriage fell apart, my work life started to collapse as well. My employment contracts dried up, my part time job disappeared and I was left unemployed. The hole I was sinking into became bigger and darker each day. I saw my boys on the weekend and isolated myself in my little home in Davis Bay the rest of the time.

I was unable to face old friends, co-workers, and colleagues. It was just too much. From having it all together, family life, work life, and spiritual life to sweet fuck all. No family, no work, no money, nothin'…just me. I felt a complete failure. My answering machine was full to overflowing, my mail box stuffed. I was responding to no one and nothing from the outside world. I would go to the ATM machines to deposit my unemployment cheque and withdraw what little cash I had to live on. I couldn't face the tellers with my unemployment cheque in hand it was just too embarrassing.

I didn't call my family. I didn't call anybody. I just sat alone when I wasn't with Oliver and Ben. Thank God for my two boys, giving me at least one thing to live for.

This mad downward spiral continued for 6 months. Now on top of isolating myself in my home, I was keeping the curtains closed. No one was going to see in and I was certainly in no frame of mind to look out. I began thinking about drugs and alcohol. Getting drunk, getting high, just to get away from the awful feelings inside my body.

I thought of killing myself.

I remember the day clearly. It was Friday afternoon around 5:30 pm. I was peeking out my front window, looking for the boys to be driven up my driveway. I was feeling like shit and didn't know how I was going to take care of them over the long weekend, I was broke and had little food in the fridge. I was feeling the full pain of my hopeless situation and really wanting to end it all.

I was full of failure and totally depressed. All I could see was another failed marriage, another lost job. I was broke and unable to care for my children. This was not how it was supposed to be and yet here I was at the bottom of my barrel.

Pills? A knife? Carbon monoxide poisoning? How would I do it? How would I end this miserable life of mine? How would I put an end to the awful fucking pain I felt? Would I leave a note?

I desperately wanted to be free from this shit I had found myself in and suicide seemed to me the only way out.

Just as I was about to turn back into my living room with thoughts of killing myself, the boys pulled up, hopped out of the car and began happily walking up my driveway, all the while looking so glad to be joining me. In a flash I got hit with many thoughts. Is this how I want to teach my boys to deal with adversity? Is this the example I want to show them? Is this the legacy I want to leave behind?…Dad rolled up the carpet and went packing when the going got tough? Tears were pouring down my face. It felt like my entire past and my whole future came crashing into this very moment. Open the door to my boys and live, or shut them out and die.

"Hey Dad, its Oliver and Ben. Can we come in?"

The moment seemed like an eternity.

I quickly pulled myself together and opened the door. I chose my boys and life.

Oliver and Ben were running around playing—I realized I had to do something to change the direction of my life. I had to do something to show my boys how a man would face adversity, what a father would do to take care of his children. I reached into the mailbox and to my relief there was an unemployment cheque there; and a solution too.

I decided to take the boys to the bank with me and cash my unemployment cheque in broad daylight, facing the teller head on even though I was embarrassed to be collecting unemployment insurance. So we hopped into the car and headed for the credit union in Sechelt. We walked into the bank and I went straight to the teller and asked to cash my cheque. To my surprise all she did was greet me saying how glad she was to see me again, that I had been a stranger for far too long. Imagine that! All the time I was embarrassed to face them and all along they were wondering how I was.

Buoyed by my experience at the bank I went over to a friend's restaurant and sat down. Brian, the owner and my friend came over and said hi. He brought along some coffee for me and two hot chocolates for the boys. He asked me how I was so I told him.

"I'm broke, unemployed, suicidal and fucked up. I need a job and I'll do anything just to get working again!" I boldly blurted out.

"Give me a second, and I'll be right back." was Brian's reply.

When he returned he offered me full time work as a dishwasher for $8.00 an hour plus a small percentage of the tip pool. I took the job, and started Monday morning after I had dropped the boys off at school.

Dish pig I was.

It was a great experience. I worked my ass off. Never before had I worked so physically hard for such little money. Yet I was happy. I listened to great music, enjoyed my fellow workers, learned lots about the restaurant business and got to eat free food!

I saw many of my old colleagues, most of whom would not even make eye contact with me. It was strange. Six months earlier I was working with these folks as their boss. Now they didn't have the time of day for me.

What the hell was going on?

Finally one day I stopped one of them. Charlotte was having lunch there with some fellow workers. I said to her as she hurried by my dish washing station, "Hey what's up? It's me remember?"

"Of course I remember, but you're a dishwasher!" she bemoaned.

"Yes I am, but it is all I can do to take care of my kids. You got a problem with that?" was my reply. Charlotte walked away sheepishly.

I realize now that she couldn't face me because it was the awful truth of riches to rags that we all fear deep inside. I had been a big shot in the local health council and now I was a mere dish pig washing dishes for a living. There but for the grace of God go I.

I understood.

The next day Marilyn Magus, an old colleague of mine, wandered into the restaurant and asked, "What are you doing washing dishes for a living? Want to teach people how to find work?"

Two weeks later I was working full time for a community service organization leading job clubs for people on welfare! I was back in social service doing what I did best, working with people.

A year later I was accepted into a master's degree program at Royal Roads University, working for an advocacy agency part time.

Two years later I graduated with Honours and was my class valedictorian! A month after that I was in Castlegar, BC as the executive director of a non-profit agency.

And so the cycle of life goes. Riches to rags to riches to rags and back again.

In the Moment

I became a victim in my own life and let go of everything I had learned. I allowed the emotions of the day to trigger all my old negative self-talk and negative beliefs. In what seemed a moment I was back at the bottom, or so it seemed, of my barrel. I fell apart, I collapsed, I wimped out.

What I Did with It Then

Though I didn't really see what was going on I got lucky. My boys saved my life. If it weren't for them walking up the driveway that day I am sure I would have tumbled even further. I got back on my bike and started riding as I always did. I picked myself up, brushed myself off, and began once again. I didn't realize though, that I had on many levels given up my spiritual life. I had pulled away from my life of service from the heart. Now I was going through the motions from my head, back in intellectual land yet again. My deepest core had again gone into hiding.

How I Think and Feel About It Now

I realize now that it was all part of my personal growth. I had gotten comfortable in my life, fallen into a rut. My separation was another loud wake up call, as was my job loss and poverty. What I did wrong was to go back to what I knew, what was safe for me—the intellect and an administrative position in social services.

What I Would Do Differently

Had I to do it over again I would have looked much more deeply into why I had created yet another marriage failure. I had again dropped to the bottom of the barrel. I would have looked deeply into what I really wanted to do in my life, what my deepest purpose and need was in that moment. I would reach out to some friends for the support I knew I needed.

Notes to the Regular Guy's Handbook

34) Live as an example for your children.
35) A man must do whatever he can to pay his way and support his family.
36) There is always something larger than your current life waiting for you.

14
Stuck on a Mountain
Alone with God

The Story As I Remember It

I had parted ways with the non-profit society I was working for and was looking for work in the social services field. My recently acquired master's degree was in most cases working against me as the positions I was applying for did not require that level of education. A friend of mine encouraged me to begin applying for executive positions, so I did. Within a week I had several interviews and ended up landing an executive director's position in Castlegar, British Columbia. I began my new job in the late summer of 2001.

I won't bore you with all the details of the story; suffice it to say I had quietly slipped back into the safe and comfortable role of an administrator. Though my agency was a social services organization and worked to help people in need, as executive director I did not. I was an organizer, fund raiser, proposal writer, and planner. I spent my time in meetings or in my office writing proposal after proposal to raise funds to keep the agency afloat. I was safe in my mind and distant enough from real contact with people in need. I looked like I was helping while staying professionally distant.

I was shut down, living in my head with little or no feelings. My heart was closed as tight as a drum and my emotions were non-existent. It felt safe in a way to be once again on autopilot.

Though initially the job was challenging, learning new faces, places, and systems, within a couple of months I had eased comfortably into a familiar role of team leader/administrator, a role I had often played throughout my working life. A role I could play with a closed heart; a role not truly in alignment with my deepest calling.

As time wore on I got more and more into my head, my old safety zone, and much less heart connected. I had fallen back into automatic pilot mode. However having been deeply active in spiritual growth work, I was not able to stay totally asleep.

The universe sent me a wake up call on May 2, 2002.

I was heading to Chilliwack with a colleague of mine to deliver a workshop. We had just turned off the highway and were waiting at a yield sign for traffic to clear. Seconds after we stopped we were hit hard from behind and pushed into the intersection. It was a nasty rear end collision—but our car was driveable. We handled the exchange of paper work, notified the police and went on our way to the workshop. We completed our piece at the conference and drove home later that day, seemingly no worse for wear.

The next morning, however, was a totally different story. I could not even get out of bed. I was suffering with extreme headaches, a totally shut down body, severe pain in the neck, upper back, and low back.

Whiplash.

I spent all day in bed with little or no relief in the level of pain. In fact as the day went on, it got worse. I was sick to my stomach on top of the increased aching and wicked pain.

Sunday was no different.

I struggled to work on Monday and put in a half day before my staff sent me off to the doctor. I was examined and diagnosed with moderate to severe whiplash. Off to the insurance company, I went and filled a claim. The insurance process began. Believe me, on top of my injuries the nightmare I experienced in dealing with ICBC was almost too much to bear. Reports, examinations, reports, x-rays, ear, nose and throat specialists, test and more reports, audiologists, kinesiologists, massage therapists and chiropractors, it never ended.

All the while I attempted to do my job. However, I was unable physically to stay in one position for more than 15 minutes. It didn't matter if I was standing or sitting; fifteen minutes was it and I had to take a break and move. Dizziness, attention deficit, and tinnitus affected my ability to do my job. I had a difficult time hearing in meetings. I could not spend the time I needed to at the computer nor in staff meetings. I wasn't able to function at the level I used to. I was making poor quality decisions, and in the end my board lost confidence in my ability to run the agency. August 30th I was let go.

Later that winter I again woke up from my automatic pilot sleep and found myself living in an A-frame cabin on the hilltops of Glade near Nelson. I realized I was not where I was 'supposed' to be. I was hundreds of miles away from my children and friends in a town I didn't particularly like. I was unemployed and hating the whole situation. Besides, there was lots of snow on the ground and I had vowed ten years earlier never to live in snow again!

It all seemed very familiar—much like when Brigit and I separated: no friends, no money—isolated and hiding out.

Shit!

What the hell was I doing in the Kootenays? When I really opened up to my current lot in life I realized that I had to get back to Vancouver.

I had been spending time in meditation and prayer. I was beginning to feel much like I did years earlier when I had struggled with leaving my career in banking. Something again was not right in my life. I could feel it.

I recall the day clearly; it was as if I'd received a message from God delivered on a lightening bolt. "Parabhakti, get yourself back to Vancouver. Now!" I packed up what little belongings I needed and the next day I walked off the mountain top down to my Tracker, never to return to Castlegar again.

Within two days of my arrival in Vancouver I had secured a job with a social service agency in Vancouver's downtown east side. The next day I started work as a facilitator in an employment training program. A month later I was supporting my teacher Anjali at a communication workshop she was facilitating. It was based on the spiritual work I had distanced myself from for the past several years. That April I was back staffing Enlightenment Intensives and beginning to re-open my heart.

I was much closer to my children and began to rebuild my relationship with them. I spent lots of time catching up and really enjoying their company. I was also catching up with old friends. All and all I was back in 'my life' and beginning to enjoy being alive again, making a living, doing some good work and having fun with friends and family.

It felt good to be 'home'.

In the Moment

I didn't spend a whole lot of time reviewing the events that led up to my return to Vancouver and my spiritual community. All I knew was it felt great to be back doing the 'work' again, serving with my colleagues and supporting others in their personal quest for Truth.

What I Did with It Then

I just shrugged it off and got back to helping people in the Downtown East Side and to working with others on their spiritual journey. I wrote off my experience in the Kootenays and my car accident as one of life's mysteries.

How I Think and Feel About It Now

I realize now that something other than me was at work in my life. The car accident, my lost job, and the sudden and direct message to return to

Vancouver were all divinely orchestrated. I had fallen asleep at the switch again and needed some type of personal crisis to wake me up and get me back on the 'path' again. Looking back at those events, as tough as they were to swallow, they were exactly what I needed. I had fallen out of touch with my spiritual community, lost sight of my deepest purpose, and had fallen back to what I felt safe doing. I was nowhere near my personal edge, nor my real purpose. I was a long way away from serving others, staffing personal growth workshops, and helping people with their growth process.

Without these rather abrupt events I could have well stayed asleep in the Kootenay running a small non-profit organization.

Thank God for crisis!

What I Would Do Differently

Instead of jumping right back into the work I used to do I would spend some time alone looking deeply into my heart to see what it was I really wanted to do—work that would have me jump out of bed in the morning whistling. What is it that my heart really wanted to give to the world, despite what my training, education and work experience would suggest? I would find a solid group of men I could trust and ask them for help with my dilemma. I would work with the group until I became clear on what I needed to do to live closer to my personal mission.

I would not go back to the status quo.

Notes to the Regular Guy's Handbook

37) There is such a thing as Divine Intervention.

38) Stay in touch with good people.

39) Living the status quo is a slow and lingering death.

15
Back with My Children
Pain from the Past

The Story As I Remember It

I had always sent money to my first wife for our two kids. However, I was mostly a distant father. Yes, I did spend time with both David and Skye, but not nearly enough. I missed most things in their lives and had drifted miles apart from them.

I had a strong urge to get to know them better. I had no idea how they would react and decided to track them down and make the first step towards reconciliation. They both lived in Vancouver, BC

David was willing to talk—so we did slowly at first. Skye on the other hand was not sure she wanted to start anew with me and run the risk of being hurt again by her distant biological father.

As time went on David and I got to know each other. Upon my return to Vancouver he and his fiancé offered me space in their two bedroom apartment until I could find a decent place of my own. He and I renewed our relationship and began getting to know each other, having some fun along the way.

It was very different with Skye.

I had not realized how deeply my distant ways had hurt her heart. She was emotionally damaged by my actions and had lots of anger towards me. In the early goings of getting to know her she was not willing to talk with me over the telephone, email contact was all she was willing to risk. So that is exactly how we started, emails.

I recognized that she was upset with me and probably had lots of things to say that I would likely not want to hear. At any rate I said to her that she could tell me anything she wanted to about how she felt about me as her Dad. She could tell me whatever upset she had about anything I did, or things I failed to do. I gave her cart-blanche. Skye took me at my word. Week after week she let me know exactly how her life was with a distant Dad like me. All her pains and aches of not having me around came out. Me not being there for her high school graduation; not there for her first boy friend; not there for most everything that was important to her in her life.

It was unbelievably painful to read and I read on. Hurt after hurt, forgotten birthday after forgotten birthday. It was dreadful. But Skye kept writing and I kept reading. As the weeks went on we slowly began to heal our tattered relationship. She was saying what she needed to say to me, things that she had held onto for so long. I was hearing and feeling what I needed to express as a result of my failure as her father.

Finally we were able to talk over the telephone.

One magical day she dropped by David's place and we met for the first time in years. Though it was awkward as hell it was so good to see her again. As time went on we all watched hockey games together, enjoyed Skye's baseball games and generally got to know each other again.

We improved our relationships as father and children and yet we may never be fully through all the hurts and pains of a separated family. We can talk and be with each other and enjoy what life has to offer us, yet we may always have a bit of distance just because of how it was.

In the Moment

I had no idea what I was getting myself into and that was a good thing. Had I known all the pain I would be unearthing I may have left it as it was!

I knew in my heart I wanted to get to know my two eldest kids better, so I simply followed my heart and let the cards fall where they would.

What I Did with It Then

I followed my heart, stayed open and fully experienced as best I could what my two eldest children had to say. I took full responsibility for my actions and inactions with both David and Skye.

How I Think and Feel About It Now

I blew it as a father for David and Skye and yet that failure has helped me immensely with my second two children, Oliver and Benjamin. I have learned from the mistakes I made with my first family. I have not deserted Oliver and Ben at all. I stay in touch with them each week and spend time with them each month. I attend special functions at their schools and do my best to be there for them when they need me. I have stayed with them through the ups and downs of the often difficult separation from their Mom. They know I love them and it shows in how they live.

What I Would Do Differently

I would not have waited so long to reunite with David and Skye. I would act much earlier when my heart said to call and say hello.

Notes to the Regular Guy's Handbook

40) It is my responsibility as a father to stay in touch with my children.

41) Do not desert your kids, it can really fuck them up.

16
My Deeper Purpose Emerges
The Blending of Capitalism and Spirituality

The Story As I Remember It

I was working for a non-profit society in the downtown east end of Vancouver. I remember being happy to be back on the front lines working with people. The work was challenging indeed and yet that was the part I enjoyed most—helping others get through their stuff and back to living their lives more fully. To be truthful though, I had put my spiritual life in the closet and really never lived it since my separation from Brigit.

I felt a strong desire to get back to living more on my spiritual path and to reconnect with my spiritual community. I tracked down my friend and teacher Anjali and began volunteering as a staff member for the workshops she was giving in Vancouver. I also began to volunteer with WarriorSage a small personal growth company owned and operated by Satyen Raja, a friend of mine and fellow student of Anjali's.

There were two workshops, Sex, Passion, and Enlightenment and the Illumination Intensive, that were offered regularly in western Canada so I put my name forward to Satyen and offered to staff any event he was putting on. Well one thing led to another and I became very involved as a coordinator and senior staff member.

At the same time work in social services was going well, I was earning a reputation as a fellow who could get the job done. I was advancing quickly as well as getting some nice salary increases.

Things were good on all fronts.

My work life was exciting and rewarding. My volunteer life was equally amazing. I was truly enjoying being back in the swing of things working with people directly.

Satyen and I got to know each other better over the next months. We renewed our eight year old friendship. We also developed a strong working relationship though I was a volunteer living in Vancouver and he was living in Brampton, Ontario.

I was at work one afternoon, a couple of days after a conversation Satyen and I had regarding full time work for WarriorSage. We had discussed it, spoke about it, even though it seemed many months off in the future.

The telephone rang. It was Satyen. He offered me full time employment starting immediately!

I accepted his offer and agreed to start in one months time.

The rest is history, I am now vice-president and senior trainer for WarriorSage, living very much on my edge and enjoying the life that was waiting for me. And it is not the one I had planned!

In the Moment

I didn't put any attention on it yet I was once again taking a leap of faith and following my heart's deepest calling. I had a secure union job with excellent pay, good benefits, and a pension plan. Yet here I was joining an upstart event management company as a consultant with no benefits, no pension and no job security. From a dollars and sense, career point of view it looked like a pretty bad risk. However, without any hesitation I took it on.

I made the choice from my heart.

What I Did with It Then

I jumped in with both feet.

I had no idea how it would work out, what my job would look like or how much income I could make. As each day arrived I just did the job. I had no idea about actually running a small four person business in the spiritual growth field and yet day by day we got the job done and the company really flourished. Our workshops became larger each time we put one on. The demand for our work was growing rapidly.

Satyen and his family moved to Vancouver in the spring of 2004, the business really exploded. Staff doubled in one year, the number of workshops we provided tripled and the size of each workshop was much larger than the previous year.

I simply kept learning and growing with the business. I grew to be whatever the business needed each day—sometimes a clerk, or an event coordinator, other times a facilitator, or a salesman. Whatever the business, needed I became.

How I Think and Feel About It Now

I trusted myself, my deepest intuition, and in a blink of an eye made a choice that would change my life forever. I have not looked back and things have only gotten better.

If I had relied on my rational thought process I would likely still be working in the downtown east end. I realized then the truth of a Joseph Campbell quotation...

"Are you prepared to give up the life you have planned in order to live the life that is waiting for you?"

What I Would Do Differently

Absolutely Nothing!

Notes to the Regular Guy's Handbook

42) Follow your heart's deepest calling—trust your intuition.

17
The Garrett Buck Stops Here
My Father's Death

The Story As I Remember It

My Dad and I had an up and down relationship, sometimes close but most often comfortably distant. Most any topic that was not personal was safe to discuss. Sports, work, and politics were the things we spoke of most. We didn't see each other often and talked perhaps monthly. That being said I knew my Dad loved me and he knew I loved him.

I had done a lot of counseling work over the years regarding my relationship with Lloyd especially the last years before his death. I was fortunate to find a psyco-spiritual counselor who helped me delve deeply into the unresolved father issues I held tightly in my inner core. I had huge releases emotionally, physically and spiritually. I was able to let go of much of the pain I had carried over the years, pain that was a barrier between my father and I.

I continued to work through these deep personal issues and noticed several changes in my life. I was feeling like I had space around me, new space to live in, a feeling of less constriction more freedom to move. I also noticed that I was talking with Dad more often and that we began to talk about real life issues, his love of his wife and family, his sense of not really being there for his kids, his failing health and from time to time his wish for death.

It was days before my Dad's death. I had just finished another deeply healing session with Robert my counselor. The very next day my Dad called; he actually called me! We had a great talk. I had never felt so close with him, and yet we both knew it was likely the last time we would speak with each other. On some level we both felt his impending death, and yet there was more life between us than ever before. How ironic, death staring my Dad square in the face and we both felt more alive as father and son.

At the end of the call Lloyd said, "Son, thanks for staying in touch over the years, it has meant the world to me. I love you."

"I love you too Dad."

Mom called days later to let me know Dad had just died.

I had a good cry with my friend Satyen, made some changes to my work schedule, flew to Toronto, joined the rest of my family at Mom's home and began the celebration of my father's life.

Though it clearly wasn't the case for all of us, I was in the fortunate place of feeling complete and fulfilled by the last call I had with Dad. I felt I could truly celebrate his life as opposed to mourning his death. This was my personal approach to the goings on of that week—celebrate Lloyd's life fully!

We set up wonderful displays of Dad's life at the funeral home and I had a great time seeing colleagues of Lloyd's, family friends and casual acquaintances I had all but forgotten over the years. I had fun remembering all the stories and adventures my Dad was very much a part of. Lots of laughs, some tears too, but most of all fond loving memories of times with Lloyd.

We had good times at the family dinner table that week; caught up with each other's lives and all told stories we remembered as kids. Yep there were the occasional arguments about who would speak at the funeral, and who would get what, all those sorts of tension issues, but for the most part we enjoyed being together as a family again. We had come from Vancouver, British Columbia, East Tracadie, Nova Scotia, Winnipeg, Manitoba, and Ontario. We were together for the first time in ten years as a full family.

We toasted Lloyd, told his whacky jokes, and laughed often as the days went by.

The funeral day finally arrived.

We set up a memory table and picture board of Dad's life at the church. We greeted friends, relatives and family. The church was full and the ceremony began.

It was a beautiful walk through the life of Lloyd Garrett. All we children stood at the front of the church and recalled moments of our life with Dad. All highlights, a glowing commentary on the goodness of Lloyd.

Mother was most proud of her children, and celebrated the life of her husband with the grace she had always lived. Marge was at peace with Dad's death.

It was over just like that. Hands were shaken, hugs were given, and good-byes were said. It was off home for a final family meal, some more stories, a few card games, and bed.

We all headed for our respective homes over the next couple of days remembering Dad in our own ways. My way was still the way of celebration. Lloyd had lived a full and adventurous life, one worth celebrating!

I was now the senior male Garrett of my family.

In the Moment

I felt complete with my Dad, there was nothing left unsaid. I got how much he really loved me and that he had always wished well for me. I also knew that my Dad knew how much I loved him. I was glad for us as father and son. I had no regrets at all.

What I Did with It Then

I enjoyed the celebration of Lloyd's life. I allowed myself to feel his loss for sure, but I mostly felt joy for the full life he had lived and the friends he had made, friends that really loved him.

How I Think and Feel About It Now

I am glad I did all the counseling work over the years. It allowed me to open up space between me and my Dad, space that let us each see one another for the men we really were. Sure we had stuff between us as father and son, but much of it was resolved in a healthy way prior to Lloyd's death. The fact that I had cleared up much of the pain in our relationship lead to my ability to celebrate Lloyd's life rather than mourn his death.

I think that mourning is often a result of incomplete issues between people, things we wished we had done and things we wished we hadn't. Things we wanted to say but didn't and things we said that we regret.

I feel totally satisfied with my relationship with my father.

What I Would Do Differently

I would have started my counseling work much earlier and been able to more fully enjoy my father earlier on in our life together. I missed many opportunities to spend time with Lloyd because of childhood hurts I continued to hold against him and make him wrong for.

Notes to the Regular Guy's Handbook

43) Spend quality time with your father—walk a mile in his shoes from time to time.
44) Therapy and counseling really work, it is a sign of courage and wisdom to get great professional help.
45) Celebrate your Dad's life with him while he is still alive.

The Regular Guy's Handbook

1) Death is more often an opening, an opportunity, as opposed to a door closing. Embracing death, particularly one's own death, is the key to living life to its fullest. As a man, feel deeply your own death, you only have so much time to leave your legacy.

2) Asking for help and support is a sign of courage and wisdom; not a sign of weakness and failure.

3) The teacher shows up when the student is ready.

4) Trust your deepest calling in each moment and follow it.

5) Be grateful for your teachers without giving your power away.

6) In everything you do, do it 100% full on, it may be the last thing you do before you die.

7) Trust your deepest intuition.

8) As many good men have said before, feel the fear and go ahead anyway.

9) There is such a thing as Divine Grace.

10) Men have all the natural and creative ability to be outstanding lovers.

11) Spiritual Union through sex is real.

12) Never give your power away to a leader.

13) Enlightenment experiences happen by Grace and are not the exclusive domain of anyone. Union with the Truth is our natural birth right, we have simply forgotten that fact.

14) Life is not as it may first seem.

15) Never follow a leader blindly and be weary of group-think, group-speak, and group pressure.

16) Taking a personal stand based on your deepest personal values is always worthwhile doing.

17) Be prepared to stand alone.

18) Any idea you have about what enlightenment looks like or how it happens is wrong.

19) Intention is a powerful force; the feeling of determination of really meaning it can move mountains.

20) Personal change and growth is risky business. Be willing for your entire life to change.

21) Listen to your inner voice, trust your intuition, you will most often know what to do.

22) Be patient with yourself, significant change takes time. Make it a project not a chore.

23) Romantic ideas are wonderful, and be prepared for the practical issues that make them a reality.

24) Changing your life is not for the faint of heart; it takes guts!

25) Celebrate your successes!

26) There is an important place for ritual in a man's life.

27) Changing a lifestyle is more than simply changing your address.

28) Men need the support of other men.

29) Support your woman fully during pregnancy no matter what.

30) Be there for your newborn child, welcome them to their new life and do it with heart.

31) Having goals is important for a man's health. Living his purpose is a matter of life and death.

32) A man needs to take a strong stand when it comes to his family.

33) Pay attention to what is really going on in your life, notice the signals your partner is giving you—and trust your intuition.

34) Live as an example for your children.

35) A man must do whatever he can to pay his way and support his family.

36) There is always something larger than your current life waiting for you.

37) There is such a thing as Divine Intervention.

38) Stay in touch with good people.

39) Living the status quo is a slow and lingering death.

40) It is my responsibility as a father to stay in touch with my children.

41) Do not desert your kids it really fucks them up.

42) Follow your heart's deepest calling—trusting your intuition.

43) Spend good quality time with your father—walk a mile in his shoes from time to time.

44) Therapy and counseling really works, it is a sign of courage and wisdom to get great professional help.

45) Celebrate your Dad's life with him while he is still alive.

Index

About WarriorSage

The Path of The WarriorSage is for those who want their personal and spiritual growth fast, and without the 'fluff' of New Age thinking. It is for you if you are willing to do what it takes to really make a huge difference in your life, and eventually in the lives of those you love, and beyond that even to serving the world open with your Awakened WarriorSage heart, skills, and insights.

The Warrior within You is that part of you that faces, feels, and moves through your fears with Courage, Openness, Honesty, Humility, and Heart, and does whatever it takes, despite obstacles, to realize your goals.

The Sage within You is that part of you that, with one foot in the World and one foot in the Mystery, is able to play, laugh, and love through life.

The WarriorSage within You is that part of you that lives with the Intention, Courage, Action and Endurance of the Warrior combined fluidly with the Humour, Transcendence, Wisdom and Love of the Sage.

www.warriorsage.com
(800) 815-1545

Spreading the Word

I wrote this book with the sole intention of helping regular guys on this planet live a fuller, richer life based on some straight forward spiritual practices. I wanted men to realize and experience that life can be full of action, purpose and deep love. I wanted the regular guy to know a great spiritual life includes everything and that it is all available now.

I also wanted to teach men how to use their life as fuel for their own personal evolution—to turn towards their life crisis instead of turning away from upset, how they can learn and grow from it, not retreat or recoil.

The tools and techniques in this book are helpful for men. They are practical and based on real life. The tools are useable now and not based on new age pyscobabble!

If you have found benefits from reading this book help me get it out to other men, the more men that read this book and get involved in our other work the better. There is a path that men can follow – a path that will lead them directly to the hero they actually are. The hero they are dying to be.

Reading this book may be their first step along this path.

If you have friends who are in a rut financially, sexually, spiritually or passionately do not delay—get this book off to your buddies and friends, don't hold back or wait for the right time.

If you have men who want to have more passion, power and drive in their lives take a chance and send them a copy of Men Read This.

If you have men who want a safe place to grow in with strong masculine loving support put your name in the front of the book and pass it along to your buddies, it could be the best thing you have ever done for them.

OK Now What Do I Do?

Personally I don't believe in wonder books or lifesaving workshops—they in and of themselves don't work. I have found this to be true in my own life. I have read hundreds of books and taken scores of workshops. But what really worked for me was when I began to take the information and apply it in my life.

So you have read my book and learned a few things about how you can lead a more passionate life full of personal freedom and love. That's great, and don't leave your insights, understandings and learnings in the book by your bedside. Begin by taking action in your life now...

Here is what you can do next.

The pages that follow include many amazing gifts for you to take full advantage of. There are two amazing gift certificates and a remarkable one-year offer.

Sex, Passion and Enlightenment Two Day Introductory workshop, with a tuition value of $697.00 per person is offered to you and a guest absolutely FREE. Here are several benefits that you will receive by attending the introductory workshop in your area;

The Illumination Intensive Five Day program with a tuition value of $1,997.00 is yours tuition FREE. All you are responsible for is the cost of your meals and accommodation plus a small administration fee. This world class event has seen hundreds of people...

The value of these gifts is $3,390.00!

Don't delay as these two workshops will help you change your life for the better.

Call our office today and register for both programs!
WarriorSage Inc.
(800) 815-1545
You must act on this offer before December 31, 2006.

Become a WarriorSage Ally!

Help us Transform fear into Courage, restriction into Freedom and separation into Love!

Think of friends, family members, co-workers, colleagues, groups and other contacts you know that would benefit from learning the critical dynamics of having successful loving relationships, or are at a place in their lives where they are asking the inevitable questions... "Who Am I?", "What is the Meaning of it all?" and "What is my True Purpose?!"

Anyone you know who is ready to have real personal and Spiritual growth "in a hurry"! As an Ally we need your help to reach out to the people you know, love and want the best for. Because we don't do any advertising, YOU are the only way the people you care about will find out about WarriorSage!

It's a fact. Your friends, family and associates will only hear about WarriorSage if you tell them about it! You probably heard about us from a friend yourself.

With WarriorSage you'll see how quick and easy it is for you to refer people with our Gift Certificates, Special Invitation Cards, and TeleClasses. You'll get rewarded for the people you invite to a Free Introductory WarriorSage Event, who enroll in one of our continuing programs!

The Benefits of being a WarriorSage Ally

✓ You'll Earn CASH and Special Bonus Prizes!
✓ You'll Get PAID helping others achieve their Relationship, Personal and Spiritual dreams!
✓ You'll get all the support tools you need to help you refer easily and powerfully!
✓ You'll create an amazing community of like minded friends who support each other in growing!
✓ Your friends will be forever Grateful for your Gift!

So here is what you do next...

1) Buy enough copies of this book so you can give each key man his own personal copy.
2) Put your name in the front of this book.
3) Give a copy of the book to each of your key guy friends and have them read it cover to cover.
4) Get together with them and have them call our offices and take advantage of the three gift certificates found in this section of the book.

WarriorSage Inc.
(800) 815-1545

5) Make sure they give our office staff your name as the person who has referred them and you will be paid once they have purchased and complete one WarriorSage Program.

Here Is Another Step You Can Take Immediately

As I said I don't believe in the wonders of a book or a weekend workshop. I do believe in regularly getting together with men who will keep you on track, men who will support your bigness not you playing small.

Anthony Robbins did a lot of research on why some people made huge progress after taking his workshops and why others didn't. You know what he found out? What made the difference in people's growth was who they hung out with after the darn workshop!

This is why I am making you another awesome offer... The League of the WarriorSage Men. It is an amazing one-year curriculum-based series of monthly men's meetings with guys like you who simply want a better life. Men who want the company of other good men. Men who are willing to support each other in creating more money, more personal power, decisive action, and more passion.

The regular tuition for this life enhancing men's curriculum is $1,497.00 and it is worth every penny of it. If you sign up before December 31, 2007 you will get this awesome program for **ONLY $297.00!**

- ✓ Really see how your work, business and financial life grow exponentially as you learn to release and galvanize your Spiritual Masculine Essence.
- ✓ Build deep progressive bonds with other men who not only will become your friends, but will become your spiritual Allies who will hold you accountable to live your deepest realization and Heart goals fully!
- ✓ Learn ongoing practices to uncover your deepest passion, Spiritual Depth and Life Purpose and to live from these deepest realizations.

The Gift of Enlightenment

yOU HAVE JUST BEEN GIVEN ONE OF THE MOST PRECIOUS GIFTS THAT ANYONE COULD EVER GIVE YOU !

FREE TUITION VALUED AT $1997 TO ATTEND

The Illumination Intensive 5 Day Workshop

When you attend this talked about seminar, you'll discover who You are… and how you can live in your Deepest Truth.

This extraordinary FREE scholarship is valid only for people who have never attended a WarriorSage Illumination Intensive and is limited to your tuition. You are responsible for your meals and accommodation.

To see if you qualify please call the WarriorSage office at 800/815-1545 or 604/534-0616 for conditions and course registration details.

Satyen Raja, President
WarriorSage